Saul, Saul, WHY Do You Persecute ME?

†

Man versus God

Deacon Norman Alexander

www.deaconnormanalexander.com

SAUL, SAUL, WHY DO YOU PERSECUTE ME?
Deacon Norman Alexander

Copyright 2014, Deacon Norman Alexander

No part of this book may be reproduced, stored in a retrieval system, or transmitted by any means, electronic, mechanical, photocopying, recording, or otherwise, without written permission from the author.

Editors: Dr. Marc D. Baldwin and Dr. Kevin of
http://edit911.com
Graphic Designer: Debbi Stocco, MyBookDesigner.com

Cover image credit: © Sedmak | Dreamstime.com - Vienna - Paint Of Conversion Of St. Paul From 19. Cent. In Augustinerkirche Or Augustinus Church Photo

Scripture quotations are from THE NEW AMERICAN BIBLE

paperback ISBN 13: 978-0-9912011-2-9
hardback ISBN 13: 978-0-9912011-3-6
ebook ISBN: 978-0-9912011-4-3

For information regarding permission, write to:
Permissions Department
5854 Sun Cove #1
Memphis, TN 38134

Or contact via website:
www.deaconnormanalexander.com

Table of Contents

Introduction 7

PART ONE

Israel 13
    THREE PLAGUES 13
    SEVEN PLAGUES 17
    THE SACRAFICE – FIRST PASSOVER 20
    PHARAOH PURSUED ISRAEL 24
    CROSSED OVER 28
    THREE-DAY JOURNEY 32
    FORTY YEARS 35

PART TWO

King Saul 43
    THREE SIGNS 46
    SEVEN DAYS 50
    THE SACRIFICE 54
    SAUL PURSUED DAVID 57
    CROSSED OVER 60
    THREE-DAY JOURNEY 63
    FORTY YEARS 66

PART THREE

Jesus Christ 73
    THREE SIGNS 78
    SEVEN SIGNS 82
    THE SACRIFICE 92
    THE JEWS AND ROMANS PURSUED JESUS 98
    CROSSED OVER 102
    THE THREE-DAY JOURNEY 106
    FORTY DAYS 110

PART FOUR

Saul of Tarsus 119
- THREE TIMES SET APART 119
- SEVEN DAYS OF CREATION AS IN SEVEN CHAPTERS 122
- THE SACRIFICE 129
- SAUL PURSUED JESUS 134
- CROSSED OVER INTO THE THREE-DAY JOURNEY 137
- FORTY YEARS 139

"Saul, Saul, Why Do You Persecute Me?" draws mainly from four books of the Bible: The Book of Exodus, The First Book of Samuel, The Gospel According to John, and The Acts of the Apostles. All quotes are from the New American Bible.

Readers who are not familiar with these Scriptures would benefit from reading them. "Saul, Saul, Why Do You Persecute Me?" has the potential to draw readers into the biblical accounts of history, and is most meaningful when these four

Books are deeply engrained in the mind of the reader.

† Introduction

WHEN POPE BENEDICT XVI FIRST announced the year of St. Paul, many welcomed it with considerable enthusiasm. I for one recognized it as an opportunity for the church to explore new means of communication and evangelization. St. Paul, one of the greatest theologians in the church, should inspire everyone interested in the study of sacred Scripture. I committed myself to study with the hopes of attaining deeper understanding of St. Paul's teachings. I saw some parallels in the lives of St. Paul and King Saul, the first king of Israel, so it seemed like the right time to delve deeper into the meaning of these similarities.

Pope Benedict XVI declared June 28, 2008 to June 29, 2009 a Year of St Paul in celebration of the 2000th anniversary of the apostle's birth. It is reckoned that St Paul was born between 6 – 10 A.D. The Holy Father explained that: *'The Apostle of the Gentiles, who dedicated himself to the spreading of the good news to all peoples, spent himself for the unity and harmony of all Christians. May he guide us and protect us in this bimillenary celebration, helping us to advance in the humble and sincere search for the full unity of all the members of the mystical body of Christ.'* To read more visit: http://www.vatican.va/holy_father/benedict_xvi/homilies/2007/documents/hf_ben-xvi_hom_20070628_vespri_en.html

Pope Benedict announced the jubilee year dedicated to St. Paul on June 28, 2007, the evening of the feast of Saints Peter and Paul, providing a year of preparation. The jubilee year meant there was a plenary indulgence offered for those who were willing and able to meet the requirements, which included a visit to the four major basilicas in Rome. At minimum, if one were not able to make a pilgrimage to Rome, we were still encouraged to study the writings of St. Paul and meditate on the events of his life.

As I meditated on the life of St. Paul, it became obvious there was a connection between St. Paul and King Saul. Of course, they were both from the tribe of Benjamin. However, that was only the beginning of a journey, fascinating and rich in detail. St. Paul was a chosen vessel of God from the beginning of time. A stream of events began with the earliest mention of Israel in salvation history, and led up to St. Paul's martyrdom and canonization.

The conversion of Saul of Tarsus had more to do with the conversion of a people than with the conversion of one man. Everyone redeemed by Christ enters into a special relationship with Christ, but the tribe of Benjamin is like the patriarch Benjamin. For example, when Joseph reunited with his brothers in Egypt he gave his brother Benjamin five times more food than he gave the others. Joseph was especially fond of his brother Benjamin. Jacob is the father of all twelve sons, but Joseph and Benjamin are the only sons of Jacob and their mother Rachel.

I would like to share some thoughts and insights about a thread of events that led to the conversion of Saul of Tarsus. Sometime after his conversion *the Holy Spirit said, "Set apart for me Barnabas and Saul for the work to which I have called them. Then completing their fasting and prayer, they laid hands on them and sent them off"* (Acts 13:2). After Saul was set apart by the Holy Spirit, he was no longer referred to as Saul in the Scriptures; he became Paul. Once the church canonized him, Christians began to refer to him as St. Paul.

St. Paul is a giant figure in the church, and one of the great heroes among the saints. The writings of St. Paul helped define how the church would be governed in the future. He was an apostle, yet he made it clear that he was the least of the apostles because he persecuted Christ. His life is a testimony that God is forgiving. The Lord forgave him, and enlightened him with the truth. He was privileged to serve God, consecrated in the truth. Some of the greatest figures in the Bible sinned against God, yet when they were humble enough to repent, God allowed them to return to service, and even places of honor. It is not practical to expect such forgiveness from earthly rulers; it is almost impossible to win back their trust. This greatly differentiates the Kingdom of God from the kingdoms of this world.

Once Saul of Tarsus became an apostle of the Lord,

meaning one sent by Jesus, he became a great leader in the church. Called "the apostle to the Gentiles," he clearly demonstrated that the church is apostolic. The holy Catholic Church is missionary, and this was exemplified by the missions of St. Paul. The church is a kingdom; she is a kingdom ruled by kings, and the King of Kings, Jesus, is supreme ruler of all. She is also a family, because she is mother to the children of God.

St. Paul was a Jew and a Roman citizen. He was a Pharisee who lived among the Greeks. King Saul and St. Paul were both Israelites from the tribe of Benjamin, but they had different reputations. Scripture tells us, *"There was no other Israelite handsomer than Saul, he stood head and shoulders above the people"* (1 Samuel 9:2), an apparent contrast to St. Paul who referred to himself as the least of the apostles. Even his name, Paul, means "little."

Let's begin viewing the story from the time of Moses' confrontation with Pharaoh's magicians. From Israel's story of redemption, we will move on to the story of Saul when he was anointed as king of Israel. The next section will reveal Jesus our Redeemer and his relationship with a fallen people. Finally, we will see how St. Paul the redeemed was restored to a place of honor.

Three Plagues

Seven Plagues

The Sacrifice - First Passover

The Book of Exodus

Pharaoh Pursued Israel

Crossed Over

Three-Day Journey

Forty Years

ONE

✝ Israel

THREE PLAGUES

ISRAEL, AN ALIEN PEOPLE IN a foreign land, cried out to God for freedom. The Lord heard the cry of the Israelites, reached down from heaven with great power, and set them free from the bondage of slavery in Egypt. When Moses approached the Pharaoh about letting the Israelites go to offer sacrifice to their God, *Pharaoh answered, "Who is the LORD, that I should heed his plea to let Israel go? I do not know the LORD; even if I did, I would not let Israel go"* (Exodus 5:2).

This bold statement is the epitome of pride and rebellion. That a creature would speak this way about our Creator reveals how far humanity is able to fall from grace. It reveals that we have joined the fallen angels in a rebellion that is not only futile but also destructive. It is a type of self-destruction that spreads itself as a cancer. The normal cells when they become old or damaged will die and be replaced with new cells, but the cells that refuse to die compromises the life of the whole body. These cells become sick and malformed. God did not create human beings to live only in the natural or the animal kingdom, where survival of the fittest preserves the species. On the contrary, we are of an eternal kingdom. The strong and dominant are responsible for nurturing the weak so they may also become strong enough to complete their journey, but everyone must accept death as the way to new life.

This happens only in a society that acknowledges the one true God. The people of this society will have no strange gods among themselves. The society that has strange and foreign gods will enslave the weaker members. They will provide a luxurious lifestyle for themselves at the expense of the most vulnerable members of society. The Israelites suffered this type of enslavement. This story affirms the old adage that he who has the gold makes the rules. The Egyptian government enslaved the Hebrews in a form of double slavery. The slave's only purpose was to provide for the needs of the slave owners. There was a permanent stigma that prevented the Hebrews from becoming citizens in the Egyptian culture, and they had to live in a perpetual state of segregation. Their only hope was to return to the God of their fathers: the God of Abraham, Isaac, and Jacob. The Israelites cried out to God and he heard their cry. God responded by sending a judge, Moses, to free them from slavery in Egypt.

When Moses had the first standoff with Pharaoh's magicians, it began with three plagues. The first miracle that Moses and Aaron performed was to turn water into blood.

More than likely Moses began to understand what God meant when he said to him *"See! I have made you as God to Pharaoh, and Aaron your brother shall act as your prophet"* (Exodus 7:1). When Aaron took his staff and stretched his hand over the waters of Egypt, their streams, canals, and pools became blood. The fish of the river died and the water became polluted. Pharaoh's magicians were able to do the same thing. Pharaoh was not impressed and remained obstinate. He would not let the Israelites go.

Next, God told Moses to have Aaron hold his staff over the river so that frogs came up out of the river and streams onto land, and Pharaoh's magicians were able to do the same thing. Pharaoh remained obstinate and refused to let Israel go.

For the third miracle, God told Moses to have Aaron stretch out his hand with his staff and strike the dust so that it turned into gnats. When Pharaoh's magicians tried to do the same thing, they were unable to mimic this miracle. *The magicians said to Pharaoh, "This is the finger of God"* (Exodus 8:15). Although it was Moses and Aaron who were performing the miracles, it was actually God who accomplished all of these great feats. Pharaoh's magicians submitted to defeat when they realized it was the finger of God that had come upon them.

These events contrast with the creation story in the first chapter of Genesis. In the beginning when the Spirit of God hovered over the waters, darkness covered the abyss. *Then God said, "Let there be light"* (Genesis 1:3). This was opposite of the story in Egypt when the water was turned into blood, because now the light has been changed into darkness. Darkness does not support life, and all the fish died. God has power over death and he revealed this truth to Pharaoh. Yet, the magicians in Egypt seem to have power in death also. It is easy to take the life of another, and those in authority have power to condemn others to death. Pharaoh had all the Hebrew baby boys in Egypt put to death and thrown into the Nile River. When God turned the waters of the river into blood, it did not change Pharaoh's heart. He was not moved to repent of his sinful acts.

The second miracle, when frogs infested the land, revealed God has command over creatures. This meant physical bodies and spirits. The Egyptian magicians evidently had power to accomplish the same thing. Not surprisingly, the magicians turned to spirits to have control over the physical world. Here we see a contrast in reference to the second day of creation when God separated the waters above from the waters below. What lived in the waters below came up unto the land. These spirits were commanded to come up from below as from the abyss.

The third miracle revealed that there is only one God. When the dust was changed into gnats, Pharaoh's magicians were not able to do the same. Only God can create life as on the third day of creation. In the third miracle, there was no contrast with the third day of creation except that human beings tried to accomplish what only God can accomplish. The magicians must finally admit that there is only one God, and the God of Abraham, Isaac, and Jacob has inflicted Egypt with these plagues.

†

SEVEN PLAGUES

After the first three plagues, Pharaoh was not willing to let the Israelites go free. Moses and Aaron were God's ministers, and the Pharaoh was the spokesman for the gods of Egypt. God brought a series of plagues upon Egypt, and after each plague, Pharaoh knew he was defeated and overpowered, but he hardened his heart and became obstinate. After all the plagues, it was only the death of the firstborn that convinced Pharaoh to let the Israelites go and offer sacrifice to their God. All of the firstborn of Egypt died, including Pharaoh's firstborn. But death passed over all the firstborn of Israel.

I spoke of a pattern of three temptations occurring at different times in the Scriptures, but there is another pattern I would like to highlight, which is that of being tested for a duration of time. An example of this would be when Daniel, Hananiah, Mishael and Asariah were in Babylon and given only vegetables and water for ten days. *After ten days they appeared healthier and better fed than all of the young men who ate from the royal table* (Daniel 1:15). These young men were faithful to God and would not defile themselves with the food provided by the king of Babylon. Because of their fidelity to God after being tested ten days, they were healthier than those who ate from the king's table. They were also superior mentally and spiritually and proved better suited to enter the king's service as advisers. *In any question of wisdom or prudence which the king put to them, he found them ten times better than all the magicians and enchanters in his kingdom* (Daniel 1:20).

Moses and Aaron were proven wiser and more prudent than the magicians in Egypt, and after the tenth plague all the firstborn of Israel were healthy enough to survive the attack of the angel of death. The Israelites were wiser and more prudent than the Egyptians and they knew to remain in the houses with the blood of the lamb on the doorpost and lintels. The ten plagues may be considered the ultimate test, because the wisdom and prudence that comes from God makes one healthy enough to survive death.

However, death did not pass over the firstborn of Egypt. All the firstborn of Egypt, of man and beast alike, died. Pharaoh and his gods could not save anyone from death. The king of Egypt provided for his subjects, and the Egyptians ate well but still died. The spiritual food of their religion did not give wisdom or prudence to discern how to avoid death on the night of Passover.

We may speak of the ten plagues as a time of being tested, and the Egyptians did not survive this test. Yet, it is important also to recognize the first three plagues as separate from the last seven plagues. The first three plagues proved that only God is able to give life. There is but one God, and the magicians of Egypt realized they were no match for the Almighty God. Pharaoh however was not convinced that he should give in and let the Israelites go and offer sacrifice to their God. He was holding on to some false hope, that if he endured long enough, something might work in his favor.

At the same time, the reality was that Pharaoh could not

give in, even if he wanted to. No one repents without the grace of God, and here in this scenario God has hardened Pharaoh's heart. The king of Egypt did not receive the grace to submit his will to God. What he did receive should have been enough to make a believer out of anyone. He was forewarned what God would do if he didn't let Israel go and worship Him. He witnessed everything predicted having come true. And when he asked Moses to pray for him, Moses did so, and God stopped the plagues. Pharaoh was given divine revelation. Should that have been enough to bring him to repentance? Obviously, it was not enough. It has been proven throughout salvation history that the truth revealed to a person in rebellion does not bring them to repentance. It may instill fear or make the person more obstinate. In Pharaoh's case, he became more hardened.

Again, I would like to relate to the creation story in Genesis. This time the contrast was destruction in Egypt as compared to construction in the creation account. The Genesis story began with God building a dwelling place able to support life. What happened with the seven plagues was chaos and destruction. It is easy to take for granted that everything in nature works together in an orderly fashion. We may even begin to think that nature takes care of itself, and this is partially true.

However, the reality is that a certain power sustains all things in creation. Creation itself does not have intelligence to recreate and keep itself in perfect order. The power that holds all things in place is the Almighty God. He created life and sustains life. Without God, there is no life, only death.

There would be no order, only chaos. No self-perpetuation would occur, only destruction and decay as we see in the seven plagues. The plagues are a glimpse of what happens when God allows nature to take care of itself without the intelligent ordering of God. Nothing works, as it should on its own. It is God who ensures that all things work properly.

When God allows humanity to depend on the false gods that it has chosen to serve, then we have the chaos seen in the seven plagues. The false gods do not have the power to hold creation in existence or establish and sustain order. It is because of the love and mercy of God that He continues to sustain creation even though we continue to serve false gods and reject our Creator. God did not allow total destruction, because his intentions are to save humanity. The judgment was on the gods of Egypt, not necessarily the people.

In the creation account of Genesis 1, on the seventh day God rested from all his work. The firstborn of Israel entered God's rest during the seventh plague, because they passed over from death to life. The firstborn of Egypt did not pass over into life, but entered death. This death implies separation from God.

†

THE SACRAFICE – FIRST PASSOVER

What was it that saved the firstborn of Israel from death? Was it the blood of the Passover lambs? The blood was put on the doorposts and lintels of the homes, and the angel of death did not take the life of anyone within the homes. The Passover was the acceptable sacrifice God commanded the Israelites to offer. Israel was saved by means of a religious liturgy. The sacrifice had to be offered in the exact manner that God commanded; otherwise, it would not be acceptable to God. The Egyptians had their own worship and their own gods, which could not save them from death. But the Israelites, who cried out to the living God had the gift of life restored to them. This was the first Passover for the Israelites, the beginning of their pilgrimage after being set free from slavery in Egypt. They began their pilgrimage out of Egypt to the land of Canaan, during the feast of unleavened bread.

Israel is now a priestly people; they are a nation and a kingdom of priests. The slaves have been set free to become royalty, and have actually taken the place of the slave owners. The Egyptians had the role of priesthood when they were blessed to provide food for the whole world. As beneficiaries of God's bountiful blessings, they had the responsibility to be good stewards. The world was in a famine, but Egypt had enough grain to provide for everyone in the world. Joseph, the son of Jacob, had the food distributed to everyone that came to buy food. However, the Egyptians forsook their duty to God and enslaved those who were put under their care.

The Egyptians were not faithful in this ministry, and enslaved the Hebrew people by preventing them from worshiping God. We can assume the Hebrews were allowed to worship the gods of Egypt. Regardless, we know from

Scripture that Pharaoh would not allow them to go on a three-day journey in the desert to offer sacrifice to God. The worst form of slavery is when people are not allowed to worship God.

When the Almighty freed the Israelites, it was celebrated by means of a religious liturgy. This first Passover marks the end of slavery for the Israelites, and the beginning of their role as a priestly people. It was the end of the Egyptian's role as priests, with the death of the firstborn signifying the end of an era. The Israelites however did not lose any firstborn, human beings or beast, and they were raised from slavery to royalty. They became a holy nation and a royal priesthood, distinguished from all the nations of the world. Their priests and sacrifices were acceptable and on the night of the first Passover they began to offer sacrifice and worship God, as he required.

True freedom is being free to do what is good, which is to worship God and keep his commands. Moses first demanded that Pharaoh let Israel go and worship God. It is interesting that the emphasis was not on releasing them from hard labor, but allowing them to worship God. From this analysis, we can conclude hard labor was not true slavery but a means of carrying it out. The hard labor was first to limit their number of births; to prevent the boys, in particular Moses, from being born. It was an attempt to eliminate the possibility of priesthood, and thus prevent Israel's communion with God. There would be no priesthood, no sacrifice, and therefore no communication.

Israel must be free to worship God, and their freedom

began with the first sacrifice. The Passover lamb and the unleavened bread were symbols of the beginning of physical freedom, and the start of a pilgrimage toward spiritual freedom. Of course, Pharaoh refused to let Israel go, stating that he did not know God and would not obey him.

It is difficult for a so-called deity to come to terms with his mortality. How could Pharaoh continue to rule his people if he admitted that he was only human as they were? Their religious belief system was threatened, and Pharaoh's word would not have the authority it once had. If the Egyptians believed Pharaoh was a deity; a descendent of a god, then his word was superior to the words of men. It was difficult for Pharaoh to accept the reality that there is only one God, the God of the Israelites. To accept that he and all false gods were powerless before the Almighty God was to admit that they had been living a lie. If he was deceived about whom he was, that would mean he was being used to deceive his followers.

He admitted when he lost a battle, but would not concede to losing the war. He was not able to repent because God hardened his heart. After each plague, he became obstinate and changed his mind about letting Israel go free. The last plague convinced Pharaoh to let Israel go. The beginning of a new era is marked with the Israelites offering sacrifice to God. They begin to worship in freedom, by obeying the commands of God. God has determined the means of worship, and this is the acceptable sacrifice. Priest and sacrifice belong to God and are consecrated to him. The Egyptians gave up their place as ministers of God by worshiping false gods and forcing others to do the same.

†

PHARAOH PURSUED ISRAEL

By the time the Israelites reached the Red Sea, Pharaoh and all his military were charging toward them with the intent of killing or enslaving them. When the Israelites faced the Red Sea with the Egyptians behind their backs, in great fright they cried out to God. Moses tried to console the people, telling them that God would save them. *Then the LORD said to Moses, "Why are you crying out to me? Tell the Israelites to go forward. And you, lift up your staff and, with hand outstretched over the sea, split the sea in two, that the Israelites may pass through it on dry land"* (Exodus 14:15,16). When Moses lifted up his staff, the Red Sea parted, allowing the Israelites to cross over on dry land.

It was the beginning of a new creation. When God instructed Moses to part the Red Sea, the Israelites had light. The Word of God is wisdom and light to those who obey. God separated the waters for them as he did on the second day of creation. He created a sanctuary that was livable and had everything needed to sustain life. On the first day of creation, God gave light. On the second day, he separated the waters with the firmament, thus providing the second most essential need to humanity; air to breathe. The Israelites received the breath of life when the Red Sea parted. Initially they were engulfed in the darkness of a great abyss; behind them, death by the hand of Pharaoh's military, before them, death by drowning in the Red Sea. But God gave them light, and the light is God's presence; the grace needed to receive the breath of life. Later, as on the third day of creation, God gave them water to drink, and, at last, when they complained of dying of famine, he gave them food to eat.

Up to this point, I have not mentioned priests, prophets, and kings in the same breath. It was the central and overriding theme in the book *The Hidden Life of Jesus*. It is time to revisit this theme, not to translate the complexity of sacred Scripture into something simple or embrace any form of minimalism, but as a reminder that this theme is always present in the history of salvation.

God sent the prophet Moses to speak to Israel and to Pharaoh. Moses was commissioned to speak the Word of God to slaves and slave owner. He was the voice that made the Word of God audible. That is the role of every prophet. Moses also spoke to God on behalf of the people. He proclaimed the Word of God when he told Pharaoh what would happen to Egypt if Pharaoh refused to let Israel go free. He also spoke to God on behalf of Pharaoh whenever Pharaoh asked Moses to pray for him. Each time, God heard Pharaoh's plea when spoken through Moses. God spoke through Moses, and heard the people through Moses, when Moses interceded for them.

During the ten plagues, the office of prophet overshadowed the office of priest, although the priestly function of Aaron was apparent because he was Moses' spokesman. Aaron ministered as priest within the jurisdiction of assisting the prophet, Moses. Thus, a priest is always a prophet, and every priest has his jurisdiction within which he ministers as prophet. However, a prophet such as Moses does not have any jurisdiction other than under God. He may offer sacrifice and speak the Word of God anywhere the Creator directs.

After the ten plagues, the office of priest became more apparent because we associate priests with offering sacrifice. Earlier, Moses' role as prophet overshadowed Aaron's role as priest, mainly because, up to the night of Passover, the story was about destruction. God gives life through the priesthood. It was only after the first Passover that it became obvious that God was giving life. The emphasis shifted to the priesthood because the firstborn of Israel received life and Israel became a royal priesthood. The destruction was part of the life giving process in the sense that priests offer sacrifice. One life is destroyed and another receives life in its place.

The destruction of the gods of Egypt during the plagues and finally their priests and sacrifices on the night of Passover makes way for God and his priests and sacrifices. The firstborn of Egypt were sacrificed so the firstborn of Israel may live in their place and take over their function as priest and sacrifice. This priestly function had the jurisdiction of the home where the Passover was celebrated. It did not have the jurisdiction of the ministerial priesthood. In this sense, the father was priest of the home and the firstborn became priest of the extended family whenever the patriarch died.

Since the fathers were slaves, their lives belonged to their master, and their children belong to their master, the Pharaoh. The Pharaoh of Egypt suppressed the priestly function of the father, which was to procreate and sustain the life of his offspring. The Egyptians tried to limit the number of births among the Israelites with hard labor. After this attempt failed, they tried to kill all of the baby boys of Israel. God provided a sacrifice and saved their sons, thus the priestly function of the father was restored to Israel. The Passover lamb became a sacrifice to save the firstborn of Israel. In retrospect, we realize this foreshadowed Jesus, the Lamb of God. He was sacrificed to save the firstborn of the New Israel.

Aaron was the firstborn of the ministerial priesthood. As high priest he was also representative of the priesthood; all who were saved at Passover. The priesthood of the firstborn in all families did not become the ministerial priesthood, but was more so a common and royal priesthood as the baptized are today. It was Aaron and his descendants that God chose as his ministerial priesthood. Jesus, the firstborn of God came to restore the priesthood of Adam, which is the priesthood of the firstborn. This priesthood of today offers sacrifice of bread and wine as done by Melchiezedec and by Jesus at the Last Supper.

When the Israelites fled into the Red Sea, the story shifted to a kingdom being saved by a king. At this point God does not tell Moses to have Aaron stretch his hand with his staff over the waters. Rather, God told Moses himself to stretch forth his hand and hold his staff so that the Red Sea parted. God was their king and military commander. He saved Israel, his military, from death. However, Pharaoh and his military drowned in the Red Sea. Israel became a kingdom of priests. Joshua was Moses' aid from the beginning, but it was not until later that he assumed the duty of military commander. He was never called a king, because God was their Savior.

Even so, Joshua functioned in the capacity of commander, but overshadowed by the glory of God.

†

CROSSED OVER

When Israel crossed the Red Sea, they crossed over into the spiritual realm. The military passed over from death to life as the firstborn did on the night of Passover. Baptized into the man Moses, Israel was the woman returned to the side of the man. The two have become one flesh as in a marriage, and God called this person, Israel, his son. Israel entered the light and therefore entered life. Guided by the angel of God, they were protected from those of the kingdom of darkness.

Darkness manifests itself in several ways, and each way is a reflection of its source. The source of darkness is the enemy of the source of light. Darkness has no conscience; it cannot distinguish between right and wrong, good and evil, or itself and light. However, those who dwell in the kingdom of darkness are well aware of the differences that exist between themselves and those who dwell in the Kingdom of Light. The enemy of light is not darkness, but is the ruler of the kingdom of darkness. The enemy of light is the angel who set himself against his Creator. Every manifestation of darkness is a reflection of the character of the ruler of darkness. Everyone who rules in the kingdom of darkness understands the power and authority given him or her by the devil, his or her god and king. All darkness begins with a lie. The kingdom of darkness is a kingdom of deceived and deceivers, and of oppressed and oppressors.

Death is darkness and those who belong to this kingdom rule by force. Their power resides in military might and the ability to inflict suffering and death upon their subjects. Since the kingdom of darkness is about deception, slavery, oppression, suffering, and death, those who rule in this kingdom oppose truth, freedom, support, healing and life, and all things pertaining to the Kingdom of Light.

The rulers of the kingdom of darkness cannot impose slavery and oppression without the willful cooperation of its citizens. There must first exist the deception that citizens are superior to those alienated. Thus, the lie precedes all injustices. The unjust society is able to legislate unjust laws because its citizens are willing to transfer, buy, and sell the alienable rights of the oppressed. As stated in the Catechism of the Catholic Church, Paragraph 407 - III. Original Sin *Original sin entails "captivity under the power of him who thenceforth had the power of death, that is, the devil."298 Ignorance of the fact that man has a wounded nature inclined to evil gives rise to serious errors in the areas of education, politics, social action, 299 and morals. (2015, 2852, 1888)* People will justify their actions to live with themselves. An example of this might be Luke 10:25-29: *There was a scholar of the law who stood up to test him and said, "Teacher, what must I do to inherit eternal life?" Jesus said to him, "What is written in the law? How do you read it?" He said in reply, "You shall love the Lord, your God, with all your heart, with all your being, with all your strength, and with all your mind, and your neighbor as yourself." He replied to him, "You have answered correctly; do this and you will live." But because he wished to justify himself, he said to Jesus, "And who is my neighbor?"*

Once the citizens of a society become at least half convinced that a particular group is inferior, then all injustices are possible. From the lie, "That the oppressed do not have inalienable rights, because they are not made in the image of God," derives ideologies and laws that institutionalize chattel slavery and the like.

The Israelites lived under this form of slavery in Egypt. The Egyptians found the Hebrews and their culture abhorrent. The Hebrew people were considered inferior because they were not made in the image of the Egyptian gods. Consequently, the Hebrews did not have inalienable rights. They did not possess the right to life, liberty and the pursuit of happiness, only the obligation to please their master, the Pharaoh.

Finally, God brought his people out of this kingdom of darkness. I would like to reiterate why I consider that time and place in salvation history the beginning of a new creation. It is like the first day of creation in Genesis 1:3 when God said, *"Let there be light,"* and the light separated the darkness. When the angel of God came between the Israelites and Pharaoh's military, God separated the light from the darkness. The Israelites had light and were able to see. This light was the way to life and Israel crossed the Red Sea on dry land. The Egyptian army could not see the light because they were opposed to the God of the Kingdom of Light. They were allowed to remain in darkness because they chose to, and it was their right to choose. The two kingdoms were separated and the Egyptian army perished in the darkness.

It was the classic situation where the oppressors were also oppressed, but did not recognize their oppression. Because the oppressors created their own gods, they saw themselves as superior to their gods and their subjects. Human beings exalted their own creation to the status of a god, and lowered their neighbors to the status of slaves. The kingdom of darkness has a beginning because it originated from a creature, but it has no end and is eternal as life itself is eternal. In this way, the Pharaoh and his army also crossed over into the spiritual realm but remained in darkness.

Once the Israelites crossed over, God cast a glance upon the Egyptians through the column of the fiery cloud. This threw them into confusion and they could not come out of the Red Sea before the waters came back together. They all drowned. Much like those in the cities of Sodom and Gomorrah who lived in the darkness of sin, the light from God blinded them. The Egyptian army was not able to find its way out of the Red Sea and avoid drowning, and the people of Sodom and Gomorrah could not find their way out of the cities to escape the trial by fire. They perished; no one looks on the face of God and lives.

One group crossed over into light and entered life. The other group crossed over and remained in darkness. The exodus from life in the kingdom of darkness ends in judgment. Jesus said, *"Amen, amen, I say to you, everyone who commits sin is a slave to sin. A slave does not remain in a household forever, but a son always remains. So if a son frees you, then you will truly be free"* (John 8:34-36). Jesus is the Son of God and He always remains in the household of God. He is able to free us from slavery to sin. Yet Jesus said to those trying to kill him, *"You belong to your father the devil and you willingly carry out your father's desires"* (John 8:44). If they are sons of the devil, then they will remain always in the devil's household. They must denounce their father the devil and become slaves, then cry out to God to be set free. Pharaoh and his military were not willing to become slaves, and remained in darkness until their lives ended in the Red Sea.

†

THREE-DAY JOURNEY

From the Red Sea, the Israelites marched out to the desert of Shur. They have crossed over into a spiritual realm. In Egypt, they lived in the flesh, but now they would have to put away the passions of the flesh and their attachment to sin. They began their three-day journey into the desert to offer sacrifice to God, and after three days without finding water, they arrived at Marah, where they could not drink the water, because the water was too bitter. As the people grumbled against Moses saying, *"What are we to drink?"* (Exodus 15:24), he appealed to God who pointed out to him a certain piece of wood. When he threw this into the water, the water became fresh.

It was the third day of creation when God caused the

waters below the sky to collect into a single basin. Then God said, *"Let the earth bring forth vegetation."* In other words, let the earth bring forth life. The bitter water was not suitable for drinking, so the earth must bring forth life in the form of vegetation. The piece of wood that God pointed out to Moses represented new life for the Israelites. Brought back from the point of death, Israel came to the end of their three-day journey to offer sacrifice.

With quenched thirsts, the Israelites moved on through the desert. The next essential was food, and they faced death again. They came into the desert of Sin on the fifteenth day of the second month after their departure from the land of Egypt. *Here in the desert the whole Israelite community grumbled against Moses and Aaron. The Israelites said to them, "Would that we had died at the LORD'S hand in the land of Egypt, as we sat at our fleshpots and ate our fill of bread! But you had to lead us into this desert to make the whole community die of famine!"* (Exodus 16:2-3). They looked back, and desired to taste the foods they ate when they were slaves in Egypt. God had pity on them and gave them manna to eat. Thus, the Creator provided sustenance. Israel came forth as a new creation; they became a people and a nation.

In the Judeo Christian experience, it is universally understood that the Passover was an important event. The scholastic intellectual as well as the ones who are barely familiar with the Scriptures will agree that the Passover is of great significance. Somehow, the three-day journey into the desert garners considerably less attention than Passover. It is interesting, however, that Moses first demanded that Pharaoh allow the Israelites to go on a three-day journey into the desert to offer sacrifice to God. This was the first and only command of God to Pharaoh. With this in mind, it appears that this part of salvation history revolved around the three-day journey in the desert. The freedom of the Israelites was based on whether they were allowed to offer sacrifice to God. Perhaps we do not speak of this journey much because we have little information about it. All that Scripture says is three days without water, and when they found water, the water was bitter until Moses threw a piece of wood into it and the water became fresh.

How was this part of the Hebrew experience different from the past? Was the miracle of making the water fresh greater than the other miracles? One main difference was that up to this point God has done everything on behalf of the Israelites. God, through his servants, Moses and Aaron, accomplished everything to secure Israel's freedom. The three-day journey in the desert was the first time that the Israelites themselves had to give up something. It was a three-day sacrifice of living without water. This sacrifice was actually a three-day sacrifice of dying without water. They were giving up their life in the flesh. Three days in the desert without water typically means death from dehydration.

The thirst was a purging fire that could not be quenched simply by drinking water. God alone is able to quench this type of thirst. That God gave them water when they were at the point of death reveals that God gave them life. They did not die from their thirst, because their thirst was quenched. However, if the thirst itself was spiritual, death was not possible unless it was death to sin. If the thirst was spiritual, it was a thirst for life, which is a thirst for God. If the thirst was quenched, the suffering was temporal. If the thirst were not quenched, the suffering would have been eternal. Fortunately, for the Israelites, the thirst was always quenched.

Because God freed the Israelites from slavery in Egypt, they belonged to him. It appears the vestiges of sin remained in them even after they were saved from death and freed from slavery. The thirst for life and freedom in God will be quenched once and for all when they are finally purged from all attachment to created things.

†

FORTY YEARS

The pilgrimage from Egypt to the promised land lasted forty years. Having God as their king was enough to terrify their enemies, but the Israelites continued to lack faith in God. When the twelve scouts were sent to reconnoiter the land of Canaan, ten of the scouts returned and spread discouraging reports. *They told Moses: "We went into the land to which you sent us. It does indeed flow with milk and honey, and here is its fruit. However, the people who are living in the land are fierce, and the towns are fortified and very strong. Besides, we saw descendants of the Anakim there. We cannot attack these people; they are too strong for us"* (Numbers 13:27, 28, 31). This discouraged people and caused them to be seized with fear. *All the Israelites grumbled against Moses and Aaron, the whole community saying to them, "Would that we had died in the land of Egypt, or that here in the desert we were dead! Why is the LORD bringing us into this land only to have us fall by the sword? Our wives and little ones will be taken as booty. Would it not be better for us to return to Egypt?" So they said to one another, "Let us appoint a leader and go back to Egypt"* (Numbers 14:2-4).

One year previous, Israel's military crossed the Red Sea with a wall of water on each side and suffered no casualties. Their enemies perished in the Red Sea; not one of them survived. Somehow, that was not enough to convince Israel to have faith in God. Because of their lack of faith, God decided to let them wander in the desert for forty years, that's a year for each day of the reconnaissance mission. All of the men of twenty years or more, registered in the census, grumbled against God except Joshua and Caleb. Because of this, only Joshua and Caleb from that generation were allowed to enter the promise land. Everyone else of military age died in the desert over the forty-year period.

The pilgrimage in the wilderness is rich in detail of miracles, rebellions, punishment, and mercy. Yet, for the sake of brevity and clarity, I have limited this section to three temptations charting the direction of Israel's destiny.

First, the Israelites refused to live by every word that proceeded from the mouth of God and they lived on bread alone. Israel ate manna every day for forty years. They rejected Moses the prophet and the call to be true prophets. Were they willing to subject themselves to Moses' authority, they would have fulfilled their call and kept the Law.

Second, the Israelites tempted God. *The place was called Massah and Meribah, because the Israelites quarreled there and tested the LORD, saying, "Is the LORD in our midst or not?"* (Exodus 17:7). They were a priestly people, yet questioned if God was in their midst. Later on, they overpowered the high priest Aaron and had him to make the golden calf. *"Come make us a god who will be our leader; as for the man Moses who brought us out of the land of Egypt, we do not know what has happened to him"* (Exodus 32:1). Aaron gave in to their request, and in doing so, he threw himself down from the top of the temple. As high priest left in charge of the people, he was head of the body, and the Israelite people were all members of the body. They were a dwelling place for God and there should have been no question about whether God was in their midst.

The third temptation the Israelites faced was to resist bowing down to the gods of the other kingdoms. They failed this temptation also. Balak, the king of Moab, sent messengers to Balaam to put a curse on Israel. *But God said to Balaam, "Do not go with them and do not curse this people, for they are blessed"* (Numbers 22:12). Balaam could not curse Israel and he gave voice to three oracles that blessed Israel. *While Israel was living at Shittim, the people degraded themselves by having illicit relations with the Moabite women. These then invited the people to the sacrifices and worshiped their god. When Israel thus submitted to the rites of Baal of Peor, the LORD'S anger flared up against Israel, and he said to Moses, "Gather all the leaders of the people, and hold a public* execution of the guilty ones before the LORD, that his blazing wrath may be turned away from Israel" (Numbers 25:1-4).

The God of Israel is blessed. As long as Israel remained in communion with their God, no one was able to curse them. However, the sin of idolatry put Israel in communion with gods that were cursed. Israel banished themselves from God's presence.

As mentioned in the book *The Hidden Life of Jesus*, Israel spent forty years in the desert as restless wanderers. Their experience was like the life of Cain who wandered the earth all the days of his life. They were in a place in which the soil would not give its yield to them, but God provided for them and gave them manna to eat each day. Spiritually they were still in Egypt, because they were attached to the material things of Egypt. The gods of Egypt remained in their hearts and was the cause of their rebellion. Because of this, God refused to remain in their midst. He would not dwell in the same body along with false gods. It was not possible for God to exist as one of their gods. Collectively, the people made up one person that God called out of Egypt. God revealed this when he told Moses to say to Pharaoh, *"Thus says the LORD: Israel is my son, my firstborn. Hence I tell you: Let my son go, that he may serve me. If you refuse to let him go, I warn you, I will kill your son, your firstborn"* (Exodus 4:22-23). When Israel brought back the gods of Egypt to dwell in their hearts, the temple became defiled, and God would no longer dwell in their midst.

The covenant that God made with his people was perpetual. Salvation of the people remained top priority even in times when it was not obviously so. The remnant perpetuated the plan of salvation. Those who were not of military age at the time of the census entered the Land of Canaan. They continued the work of God their fathers abandoned.

Three Signs

Seven Days

The Sacrifice

The First Book of Samuel

Crossed Over

Saul Pursued David

Three-Day Journey

Forty Years

TWO

†

King Saul

THE ISRAELITES FINALLY SETTLED IN the land of Canaan, a land flowing with milk and honey. God fulfilled his promise and began driving out the nations before them. There was one thing standing in the way of total success for the Israelites. Their success was dependent upon their fidelity to God. The covenant was a two-way agreement between God and Israel. God offered the terms of the covenant, but Israel agreed to it freely. When the Law was given to the Israelites, this covenant was ratified only when Moses *Taking the book of the covenant, he read it aloud to the people who answered "All that the LORD has said, we will heed and do"* (Exodus 24:7). It was not a covenant until God and the people agreed to the terms. By agreeing to live under the Law, the Israelites have obligated themselves to obey what is written in the Law. They were citizens of a kingdom governed by God.

All was wonderful in this great theocracy, except when Israel did not keep their agreement. This means that God would drive out the nations before them, if they kept the covenant. They would not be inflicted with certain illnesses, if they kept the covenant. Their days on earth would be long and prosperous, if they kept the covenant. We could go on and on but the point is that God is always faithful, because God is truth. It is not possible for God to be unfaithful. However, if Israel rejected God and became unfaithful, God would honor their request, and let them fight their own battles.

During the period when judges led Israel, they lost many battles to the Philistines. They suffered many hardships and lost their freedom many times to these people. One might ask, "If God was their King, why were they losing battles?" The number one problem was that the Israelites continued to disobey the first commandment by serving and worshiping foreign gods. When the Philistines, Ammonites, Moabites, or other nations attacked and defeated Israel, it was because these foreign gods could not save Israel. The Israelites would have to humble themselves and cry out to God, who always responded by sending a judge to save them. Eventually, they asked for a king to judge them. Their success or failure was dependent upon their faithfulness to God.

The Israelites had a story similar to Adam and Eve, whose lives were dependent on whether they kept the command of God. To eat from the tree of knowledge of good and evil meant death, because it was disobedience to God. As long as they lived by faith and believed the Word of God, they lived continually in peace, and without sickness or death. The moment they began to walk by their own sight and judged for themselves what is good and what is evil, the peace they enjoyed was disrupted and they began to suffer. The suffering is associated with illness, which eventually leads to death. The first woman confronted the opportunity to take her destiny out of the hand of God by disobeying the Word of God. Only one commandment to live by, and a foreign god, the serpent, talked them into disobeying that one command.

However, we should not be judgmental towards Adam and Eve, because we, the people of God during these times, are no different. Many sincere Christians obey the teachings of the Church, but not in all things. There may be one command we find difficult to obey. There may be one teaching we find hard to believe. The refusal to submit to the teaching authority of the church makes us no different from our first parents. Distrust of teaching authority is the beginning of a journey that leads away from the fullness of truth.

Yes, the Israelites were like Adam and Eve, and so are we. When Israel worshiped foreign gods, it was a rejection of the command of the true God, and a rejection of the covenant. You may also say they rejected the Word of God. To reject the Word of God, one must also reject the prophet, such as when Samuel was rejected. The Israelites were bound to the covenant only if they chose to be. However, when the Israelites asked God to save them from the Philistines, God did not abandon them, but sent a judge to save them. They called on God because they were willing to return to him, and God in his mercy always forgave their infidelity.

In Samuel's old age, his sons, whom he appointed judges over Israel, did not follow his example but sought illicit gain and accepted bribes, perverting justice. The elders of Israel came to Samuel and said to him, *"Now that you are old, and your sons do not follow your example, appoint a king over us, as other nations have, to judge us." Samuel was displeased when they asked for a king to judge them. He prayed to the LORD, however, who said in answer: "Grant the people's every request. It is not you they reject, they are rejecting me as their king. As they have treated me constantly from the day I brought them up from Egypt to this day, deserting me and worshiping strange gods, so do they treat you too"* (1 Samuel 8:5-8).

It appears the people of Israel wanted a king because they refused to give up worshiping strange gods. A king does not judge looking forward as a prophet does. A king judges looking back, and this means that a king governs in the flesh, not in the spirit. Again, I relate this to the story of the first woman, Eve, who was governed in the spirit when she followed the command given to her husband. When she rejected the prophet, it was God she rejected, giving the devil the opportunity to twist the meaning of the Word of God and deceive her. No longer did God govern her soul through the prophet. She gained independence and the liberty to be self-governed. Their descendants would be governed in the flesh throughout the centuries, because the serpent governs in the flesh, and through the flesh.

†

THREE SIGNS

It is ironic that, when they were slaves in Egypt, the Israelites cried out to God to set them free. Now they were asking to be liberated from God, their King and Savior. Their request was granted and God gave them a king. He revealed to Samuel the one he was to anoint as king of Israel. It was Saul, son of Kish, from the tribe of Benjamin. Samuel told Saul that he had a message for him. *Then, from a flask he had with him, Samuel poured oil on Saul's head; he also kissed him, saying: "The LORD anoints you commander over his heritage. You are to govern the LORD'S people Israel, and to save them from the grasp of their enemies roundabout. "This will be the sign for you that the LORD has anointed you commander over his heritage: When you leave me today, you will meet two men near Rachel's tomb at Zelzah in the territory of Benjamin, who will say to you, 'The asses you went to look for have been found. Your father is no longer worried about the asses, but is anxious about you and says, 'What shall I do about my son?' Farther on, when you arrive at the terebinth of Tabor, you will be met by three men going up to God at Bethel; one will be bringing three kids, another three loaves of bread, and the third a skin of wine. They will greet you and offer you two wave offerings of bread, which you will take from them. After that you will come to Gibeath-elohim, where there is a garrison of the Philistines. As you enter that city, you will meet a band of prophets, in a prophetic state, coming down from the high place preceded by lyres, tambourines, flutes and harps. The spirit of the LORD will rush upon you, and you will join them in their prophetic state and will be changed into another man. When you see these signs fulfilled, do whatever you judge feasible, because God is with you. Now go down ahead of me to Gilgal, for I shall come down to you, to offer holocausts and to sacrifice peace offerings. Wait seven days until I come to you: I shall then tell you what you must do." As Saul turned to leave Samuel, God gave him another heart. That very day all these signs came to pass"* (1 Samuel 10:1-9).

The Israelites were in a similar predicament in Egypt. The Canaanite nations worshiped many gods and they were naturally hostile to the Israelites. This hostility stems from the Israelites' worship of one God. The God of Israel said that the Canaanite gods were false gods, and that he would do away with them. It had more to do with spiritual beings than false gods made with human hands. The false gods made with human hands only indicates that people try to become gods, and what they create with their hands is subservient to them. Humanity becomes the creator and its god or gods are part of their creation. The idea of worshiping foreign gods began with the serpent in the Garden of Eden. This practice continues throughout history with humanity serving and worshiping the serpent and a third of the angels who followed him into rebellion against God.

The Philistines and all of the other nations in the land of Canaan desired to enslave the Israelites because they perceived the God of Israel as their enemy. Their behavior was similar to that of the Pharaoh of Egypt. The Philistines continued to make war against the Israelites to enslave them. If the Israelites were allowed to live in peace, they would have possessed the land and displaced all of the nations that worship foreign gods. The mission of the Israelites was to be a military for God. He would use them to clear out the land, and to take back what the devil had gained by deception. The Israelites would have to fight for their freedom; otherwise, they would be taken into slavery, as they were in Egypt.

The Almighty God in his infinite wisdom is fully aware that justice is not possible in a society that worships false gods. The different nations in the land of Canaan war against each other because their gods do not love one another. Because of this, it was not possible for the people to live in peace.

Some of the nations were prepared to fight to the bitter end. Why? Because like Pharaoh of Egypt, they did not know God, and even if they did, they would not obey him. That was the main reason why the Israelites were told to displace the Canaanite nations.

Once the Israelites were given a king to rule over them, their quest for freedom from the Canaanite nations, mainly the Philistines, began to look like the struggle for freedom when they lived in Egypt. Moses and Aaron began to show Pharaoh that he was powerless against the Almighty God. The first three signs that Moses and Aaron demonstrated was to turn water into blood, bring frogs out of the waters onto the land, and to turn the dust into gnats. This third miracle revealed that the God of the Israelites is the Creator, as only the Creator can bring forth life from the dust.

When Saul was anointed king of Israel, the story began with three signs. This time Israel did not have God as their king, but a man to rule over them and to judge them. The three signs revealed that although Samuel anointed Saul as king, it was God who anointed him as king. Like the first three miracles Moses and Aaron performed in Egypt, it was actually

God that worked these miracles. This was acknowledged by Pharaoh's magicians when they said, *"This is the finger of God."*

Samuel ministered as priest when he anointed Saul, because he represented God. Moses and Aaron represented God when performing the miracles in Egypt. Our priests today stand in the person of Christ when ministering the sacraments. Moses, Aaron, and Samuel exemplified how God used his priests in the Old Testament. God was made present in the lives of his people using ministers, form, and elements.

It was miraculous that Samuel knew what would occur in the future. Understandably, things are revealed to prophets that are hidden from others. Those who practice witchcraft, have knowledge and power also, but from a different source. We saw this demonstrated when Pharaoh's magicians were able to perform the first two plagues using their magical arts, but not the third. The third sign revealed God as the giver of life, and it was the Spirit of God that came upon Saul and the prophets.

†

SEVEN DAYS

After Saul received confirmation that God had anointed him king of Israel, he immediately began to fulfill his duty as commander of God's people. He began his watch as military commander fighting against the Philistines. Because of the size of the Philistine army and the danger, some of the Israelites hid themselves, and other Hebrews passed over the

Jordan into the land of Gad and Gilead, Saul, however, held out at Gilgal, although all his followers were seized with fear. The seven days of battle between Israel and the Philistines reflect back to the battle between Israel and the Egyptians.

Throughout the seven plagues, the Egyptians were helpless and the only recourse they had was to admit defeat. They had no means of fighting back against God, and had to endure all the hardships caused by the plagues. Yet, after each plague, the Lord gave them the opportunity to avoid further suffering. Pharaoh remained obstinate and held out, believing that he could endure without repentance.

One man, Pharaoh, decided to hold out no matter how much the others in his kingdom suffered. He chose to endure all that the Lord inflicted upon them. He was helpless and his people realized they were doomed. The reason why they were doomed and helpless is because the king of Israel was the Almighty God. The Lord God, Creator of the universe is all-powerful, and no one within his creation can fight against him. All that Pharaoh and the Egyptians could do was wait and see what God would do next.

Concerning the contrast between these two events, Israel had rejected God as their king, and opted to replace God with a man. When this man began to defend them as their military commander, he was apparently helpless. His predicament was similar to that of the Egyptians. The Philistines outnumbered the Israelites, and the Israelites seemed powerless against the Philistines. Saul's men were seized with fear; hid themselves, and waited to see if they were to survive the attacks of the Philistines. The Israelite army did what the Egyptians did when they were inflicted with the plagues, and King Saul did what the Pharaoh did; he held out until the end. Saul held out for the duration of the seven days as Pharaoh held out for the duration of the seven plagues. In the meantime, Saul realized that the men were slipping away from him. We can say the same thing about Pharaoh, since he went from being a god to being someone helpless before his enemy. Everyone in Pharaoh's kingdom now realized that he was powerless before the God of Israel.

Israel's first lesson after rejecting God was to see how inferior their mortal king was in comparison to God. Their new king endured seven days of exposed helplessness. He could not protect his men from the Philistines. His only recourse was to wait until the seven days had passed.

The seventh day was the day of rest, and Saul should have been able to enter God's rest. To enter the Sabbath rest is to worship God in spirit and truth. The Spirit of God had already come upon King Saul. Saul therefore was duty-bound to remain in truth. It is the true worship and fidelity that God demands from all of us. Saul did not enter God's rest, but instead sinned against the Law by offering the holocaust. By doing so he altered the course of history for his family and all of Israel.

When God gives dominion to man, it is so that God himself has dominion. The Spirit of God governs this way in the Kingdom of God. As with the first man Adam, God blew the breath of life into his nostrils and he became a living being. Likewise, the Spirit came upon King Saul when he was among the prophets, and he became a changed man. He became a living being, as Adam did. But what sustained the life of Adam was the Word of God. As long as he kept the Word of God he was able to remain alive because the Spirit of God remained in him. Adam had to keep the command; he was free to eat from all the trees in the garden except the tree of knowledge of good and evil. He had before him the way to life and the way to death. Had he chosen to obey the Word of God; he would have kept dominion over the earth. It was God who gave Adam dominion over the earth, but it was Adam's disobedience to the Word of God that caused him to lose dominion and become a slave. He also eventually had to give up the breath of life, the Spirit, which God blew into his nostrils.

God gave Saul dominion over his people, Israel. Saul would have kept dominion as king over Israel had he obeyed the Word of God. The command he was given was to keep the Law. Saul was to wait seven days until Samuel came to him. At this time, Samuel would have offered the holocaust and peace offerings for him. King Saul offered the holocaust himself and disobeyed the Word of God. Only the priests of God could offer the sacrifice. King Saul disobeyed God and lost dominion, as did Adam. Eventually the Spirit of God left Saul, and an evil spirit began to torment him. He suffered the fate of Adam, as he began to experience death.

†

THE SACRIFICE

God took the kingdom away from Saul and his descendants. The Law strictly forbids unauthorized persons from offering the sacrifice. This sacrifice was unacceptable to God, and different from the sacrifice of the Passover lambs in Egypt. God gave specific instructions to sacrifice the Passover lambs and instructed the Israelites how to offer the sacrifice. Because God demanded the sacrifice and gave orders how to celebrate the Passover, it was an acceptable sacrifice to God. Those who break the Law by offering worship in a way that God forbids are not offering worship to God, and God will not accept the sacrifice. God gave evidence to this when on another occasion Saul brought back a king and livestock that were under the ban. His reasoning was that he brought the animals back for sacrificing. *But Samuel said, "Does the LORD so delight in holocausts and sacrifices as in obedience to the command of the LORD? Obedience is better than sacrifice, and submission than the fat of rams. For a sin like divination is rebellion, and presumption is the crime of idolatry. Because you have rejected the command of the LORD, he, too, has rejected you as ruler"* (1 Samuel 15:22-23). God took the kingdom from Saul and his descendants and gave it to his servant David.

The Egyptians worshiped false gods and abandoned their responsibility to distribute God's bountiful blessings to the world. They enslaved the children of God and preferred to kill them rather than let them go free to serve God. When Israel left Egypt, the slaves were set free to become royalty. This is what happened with King Saul and David his servant. David was exalted from servant to King, and replaced Saul as commander and protector of God's people. David became king in as much as Israel became a royal priesthood.

Interestingly both King Saul and the Egyptians have committed offenses against God and the worship of God. It is a sure sign that God dictates how he is to be worshiped. We must all conform and not delude ourselves. The goal is to worship God and not self. The acceptable sacrifice such as Passover saved the life of the firstborn of Israel, and the unacceptable sacrifice did not save the firstborn of Egyptian from death, neither did it save Saul and his family.

It can be difficult at first to follow the chronological events in the life of King Saul. This will require some effort because the events are not in a linear sequence. Some things occur and, in the middle of the story, we are taken to another story at another place and time. Then the original story resumes and picks back up where it left off.

Some examples of this are in 1 Samuel 10. In this chapter, Samuel anointed Saul as king. Saul received the three signs as Samuel said. Samuel told Saul to wait seven days and Samuel would come to him at Gilgal to offer holocaust and to sacrifice peace offerings. Samuel would also tell Saul what he must do. After the three signs had been fulfilled, Samuel brought Saul before the people and read to them the rights of a king, then dismissed the people.

The story moved to about a month later when Saul came

to the rescue and defeated the Ammonites whose king had threatened to gorge out every man's right eye. After Saul proved himself a worthy commander, the people went to Gilgal and made Saul king. They also sacrificed peace offerings and celebrated the occasion with great joy, and this is how the eleventh chapter ends.

The twelfth chapter continues with Samuel giving instructions to the people and their new king. The thirteenth chapter returned to Saul fighting against the Philistines and waiting seven days for Samuel to come and offer the holocaust and peace offerings. It was at this point when the men were slipping away from Saul that he offered the holocaust. Samuel arrived when Saul had just finished this offering. *Samuel's response was: "You have been foolish! Had you kept the command the LORD your God gave you, the LORD would now establish your kingship in Israel as lasting; but as things are, your kingdom shall not endure. The LORD has sought out a man after his own heart and has appointed him commander of his people, because you broke the LORD'S commandment"* (1 Samuel 13:14).

The events do not flow in a chronological order, so it may be necessary to explain the significance of the seven days that Saul waited for Samuel. It was after Saul offered the holocaust that he experienced the death of the firstborn as the Egyptians did the night of the first Passover. After seven plagues, the ministry was taken out of their hands and given to their servants the Israelites. It did not pass on to their future generations, and this is part of the meaning of the death of the firstborn.

† SAUL PURSUED DAVID

This news upset Saul greatly, yet it did not cause him to be obedient. Saul disobeyed the command of God again, this time the Spirit of God left him. The Lord instructed Samuel to give Saul the command to make war against the Amalekites. He was instructed to kill the King of Amalek and all of the people. There was also a ban placed on all of the animals, everything in that place was to be destroyed. Instead of obeying this command, Saul brought back the king and all of the choicest animals. He only killed those animals that were worthless. From that time on the Lord did not speak to Saul; neither by prophecy, dreams, nor with the *Urim and Thummim*. The office of prophecy was taken from him. At this time, Samuel revealed to Saul that David would take his place as king.

When the Spirit of the Lord left Saul, the Lord sent an evil spirit to torment him. His servants suggested that David play the harp to sooth Saul. Saul agreed to this and, when David played the harp, Saul was relieved of the torment. This put David in a very precarious situation, because Saul had tried to kill David.

Saul could not accept the idea that his servant David would be set free from service and made king. He decided to pursue David in a similar manner as the Egyptians pursued the Israelites into the Red Sea. By trying to kill David, he was actually fighting against God. This reality did not distract Saul from his determination to kill David. He pursued David until the end of his life and although David had many opportunities to kill Saul, he would not sin by laying a hand on Saul, because Saul was God's anointed.

Finally, Saul went to a witch to consult a ghost and predict his future. Divination is one of the more serious offenses against the commandments of God and was punishable by death. He met his fate, just as the Egyptians did in the Red Sea. He saw Israel defeated by the Philistines. Saul's sons were killed and Saul was wounded in battle. However, the Philistines did not kill him; he took his own life. It was his decision to give up his life rather than let the Philistines kill him.

Saul pursued David until David was forced to live among the Philistines. He joined the Philistine army and marched as their rearguard. By forcing David to flee for his life into the hands of the Philistines, Saul had forced him into the hands of Israel's greatest enemy. Saul was pursuing David to kill him, and the Philistine army was the last place that David and his men would want to be. Surely, this should have been a death sentence for David and his men, but God protected David and his army. They lived among the Philistines and marched with the Philistine army.

When Saul forced David and his men into the hands of the Philistines, their situation paralleled the experience of the Israelites who were forced into the Red Sea. David and his army were in the midst of the Philistine army, but he and his soldiers marched through unharmed. The Philistine lords told the commander that David and his men should not be allowed to fight in their army because his loyalty would be for his people and he may try to win Saul's favor. He may perhaps turn on the Philistines in battle. In other words, it is too risky to allow David to continue marching with the Philistine army. So David and his men filed out of the ranks of the Philistine army unharmed, as Israel marched through the Red Sea on dry land.

There are two important similarities that can be made between King Saul and the Pharaoh. The first was when King Saul offered the holocaust. The second was when Saul went to a witch to conjure a ghost for him. In the first situation, the Lord did not accept this sacrifice because, according to the Law, Saul was not allowed to offer the sacrifice. Only Aaron and his descendants could offer the sacrifice. The kingdom was taken away from Saul and his descendants. Saul was the first king of Israel. He and his sons were rejected, and it was the death of the firstborn, just as Pharaoh and the Egyptians were rejected the night of the first Passover.

Saul's story is like the Pharaoh and his army that perished in the Red Sea. David, however and his army are like the Israelites because no one died or was harmed when David left the Philistine army. No one in Israel's army died, nor was anyone harmed when they crossed the Red Sea. In these two incidents, it is possible to compare the death of the firstborns and the death of the king and his military. Both Pharaoh and Saul forsook their duty to God. Each person also lost their firstborn and perished along with the military. Pharaoh's slaves became a royal priesthood to replace Pharaoh and the Egyptians. Saul's servant became king and replaced Saul and his descendants as military commander of God's people.

†

CROSSED OVER

King Saul crossed over into the spiritual realm when he visited the witch. The vision of Samuel coming up out of the grave prefigures the resurrection of Christ. Saul looked on the face of God as Pharaoh and his army in the Red Sea when God gave them a glance through the fiery column in the cloud. God gave Saul a glance, and Samuel revealed to him, *"By tomorrow you and your sons will be with me"* (1 Samuel 28:19).

The grave sin of divination is to cross over deliberately into the spiritual realm. Once Saul had crossed over, it appears there was no turning back. King Saul did not go from light to darkness. He lived in the darkness of rebellion and presumption. As Samuel explained to Saul, *"For a sin like divination is rebellion, and presumption is the crime of idolatry"* (1 Samuel 15:23). Saul's rebellious behavior led to divination. His judgment was death; he will live no more in the land of the living. He lived in darkness on this side of the grave and crossed over into darkness, which was death.

By no means are we to interpret this as Saul's eternal judgment. There appears to be a bright side to this story in that Samuel told Saul, *"By tomorrow you and your sons will be with me."* To die and be with Samuel could be a good thing, yet Samuel could have meant simply that Saul and his sons would die. Saul crossed over from darkness in the flesh to darkness in the spiritual realm. In the Old Testament, the covenant was in the flesh. The reward for doing good was enjoyed here on earth. The punishment for doing evil was suffered here on earth. There was no obsession with the afterlife as that which existed among the pagans.

Because Saul lived in darkness, when Samuel appeared and revealed his destiny, the light of divine revelation blinded him as one looking directly into the sun. The light of divine revelation was more than he could bear and he fell to the ground as one dead. He was blinded as Pharaoh was blinded in the Red Sea. He was blinded as the men of Sodom were blinded when they tried to enter Lot's house. Likewise, he was not able to find his way out of the battle with the Philistines. The Philistines overcame him as the waters of the Red Sea overcame the Egyptians, and fire and brimstone overcame the men of Sodom and Gomorrah.

Again, God separated the light from the darkness. The battle with the Philistines was darkness to Saul and his army. He went into this battle knowing that he and his sons would die. He and the Israelite army remained in darkness throughout the battle, much like Pharaoh and the Egyptian army remained in darkness in the Red Sea. In contrast, David and his army had light the whole time he was among the Philistines. David led successful raids and battles and accomplished his goals as one with sight and insight.

When the time came for David to march out of the Philistine army he did so as someone escaping death and slavery. He escaped the slavery of sin, because he would have been faced with fighting against Israel. God anointed Saul as king, and David would not lay a hand on Saul. To lay a hand on God's anointed would have been a sin. When the Philistine lords demanded that David no longer march with their army, it so happened that God overpowered them. Once again, evil men were seduced into doing the will of God. In no way would God want David to sin by killing Saul. David was in the same predicament as Israel when Pharaoh's army chased them into the Red Sea.

Israel faced death if they turned around, because Egypt's army would have killed them. If Israel went forward into the Red Sea, everyone would have drowned. When Pharaoh chased Israel into the Red Sea, he actually forced them into the light. He was seduced into accomplishing the will of God. Pharaoh's obstinacy brought glory to God. Israel was forced into the light of God and remained among the living. The Egyptian army remained in darkness and entered the abode of the dead.

This was David's story also, because when Saul forced David into the land of the Philistines he actually forced David into the light. The light was that Saul no longer pursued David because he could no longer see David. He did not see David, because David was in the light and Saul was in the darkness. Saul could not find David in the land of the Philistines any more than Pharaoh could find Israel in the Red Sea. The light gave David sight, but he needed more than light. The light allowed him to see but he also needed to be able to escape death by the hands of the Philistine army. Since Saul forced David into the Philistine army, he caused David's dilemma. If he refused to go to battle against Israel, the Philistine army would have probably looked at him as an enemy. More than likely, they would have killed David and his men. So, David went forth with the Philistines to make war on Israel. He went forth as the Israelites into the Red Sea, and, just as God parted the Red Sea for Israel, he provided a way for David to come through the Philistine army alive.

If David went to war against Israel and Saul was killed, then David would have died because of his sin. But God does not tempt anyone beyond his or her ability, but always provides a way out. God provided a way out for David to avoid sin, because the wages of sin is death. David's way out was the Philistine lord's demand that he and his men should not go to war against Israel. The light guided David, and God parted the waters for him to keep the breath of life. Saul however remained in darkness and could not see David to pursue him. Saul and his army did not keep the breath of life, because the Philistine army took it from them.

†

THREE-DAY JOURNEY

After Samuel revealed to Saul his doom by the hands of the Philistines and David marched out of the Philistine army unharmed, the three-day journey began, similar to the three-day journey of the Israelites after crossing the Red Sea. In 1 Samuel 28, Saul and his sons perished as Pharaoh and his military did in the Red Sea. Chapter 29 has David marching out of the Philistine army unharmed as the Israelites coming through the Red Sea. Chapter 30 begins with the Amalekites raiding the Negeb and Ziklag on the third day before David and his men reached Ziklag. The Amalekites took captive the women and all who were in the city, young and old, killing no one; they carried them off when they left. David's two wives and all of his soldier's wives and daughters were taken captive. *Now David found himself in great difficulty, for the men spoke of stoning him, so bitter were they over the fate of their sons and daughters. But with renewed trust in the LORD his God, David said to Abiathar, the priest, son of Ahimelech, "Bring me the ephod!" When Abiathar brought him the ephod, David inquired of the LORD, "Shall I pursue these raiders? Can I overtake them?" The LORD answered him, "Go in pursuit, for you shall surely overtake them and effect a rescue"* (1 Samuel 30:6-8).

The three-day journey to Negeb and Ziklag ended when they found their destination burned and their families taken captive. All life was gone with no means of reproduction; this was as final as death. Compare this to the Israelites who after three days in the desert tell Moses, *"Give us water to drink."* The water they found was bitter and they could not drink it. God revealed to David how to restore life to their cities by bringing back all of the captives. When the captives were returned it could be compared to the bitter water becoming sweet. The Israelites would not die of thirst and David's army would not die without offspring. The life was in the water, and the life was in sexual reproduction.

Someone else of great importance in the three-day journey was the Egyptian found in the open country and brought to David. *He was provided with food, which he ate, and given water to drink; a cake of pressed figs and two cakes of pressed raisons were also offered to him. When he had eaten, he revived; he had not taken food nor drunk water for three days and three nights. Then David asked him, "To whom do you belong, and where do you come from?" He replied: "I am an Egyptian, the slave of an Amalekite. My master abandoned me because I fell sick three days ago today"* (1 Samuel 30:11). He agreed to lead David to the raiding parties if David agreed not to kill him or return him to his master.

The rescue was successful. *David recovered everything the Amalekites had taken, and rescued his two wives. Nothing was missing, small or great, booty or sons or daughters, of all that the Amalekites had taken. David brought back everything. Moreover, David took all the sheep and oxen and as they drove them before him they shouted. "This is David's spoil"* (1 Samuel 30:18-20).

This particular insight is an important prophetic link to the story of redemption. I will discuss later in the chapter on Saul of Tarsus why I believe this three-day fast is so important. For now the man, whose name we are not given, had gone without food or water for three days during the time that David and his men were on their three-day journey. His three-day journey was as much of a sacrifice as the Israelites who traveled three days into the desert without water.

King Saul was like the Egyptians who crossed the Red Sea, and he is a slave of an Amalekite because he brought the king of Amalek back alive against the will of God. The Lord said, *"I will completely blot out the memory of Amalek from under the heavens"* (Exodus 17:14). If Samuel put this king to death and Saul and his army killed all the people, how did

God war against Amalek? Perhaps this story reveals the battle against the devil. If so, the Egyptian slave of an Amalekite is a symbol of King Saul, who was battling against God by killing his priests and trying to kill David. He was a slave to the king of Amalek and to the riches of sheep and oxen that he was commanded to destroy. He would not destroy the livestock because it was valuable to him; more valuable than obedience to God. Perhaps King Saul and his sons crossed over and are with Samuel. In the plan of salvation, his descendants would be redeemed, and the tribe of Benjamin restored to serve the Lord as the great warriors who would lead David to take back his plunder from the Amalekites.

†

FORTY YEARS

Saul ruled as king over Israel for 40 years. During this time, he had many successful battles and he fought valiantly. He is remembered as one who disobeyed the Lord and thus the kingdom was taken away from him and given to David. This is true, but there was more to King Saul than his failures. He was God's anointed and the protector of God's people. He served the Lord in that role very successfully. There was another side to Saul that made it difficult for him to obey the commands of the Lord. As a military commander, he began to fight against the enemies of the Lord immediately after he was anointed as king. About a month later, he defeated the Ammonites. *After taking over the kingship of Israel, Saul waged war on all their surrounding enemies—Moab, the Ammonites, Aram, Beth-rehob, the King of Zobah, and the Philistines. Wherever he turned, he was successful and fought bravely. He defeated Amalek and delivered Israel from the hands of those who were plundering them.*

An unremitting war was waged against the Philistines during Saul's lifetime. When Saul saw any strong or brave man, he took him into his service (1 Samuel 14:47-48,52).

King Saul's disobedience led him into a struggle against God. Many of Saul's successes were because of David, whom he had brought into his service. By the time Saul had made a second mistake by directly disobeying the command of the Lord, he realized that the Lord was no longer with him. God took the kingdom from Saul and his descendants and gave it to David. Although David would serve Saul as the captain of his bodyguard and commander of his armies throughout the years, Saul was extremely jealous of David and he feared David because the Lord was with David.

After the Spirit of the Lord left Saul and he was tormented by an evil spirit, David played the harp to relieve Saul. The king was very pleased with David and his service until David killed Goliath. *At the approach of Saul and David (on David's return after slaying the Philistine) women came out from each of the cities of Israel to meet King Saul, singing and dancing, with tambourines, joyful songs, and sistrums. The women played and sang: "Saul has slain his thousands and David his 10,000s." Saul was very angry and resentful of the song, for he thought: "They give David 10,000s, but only thousands to me. All that remains for him is the kingship." And from that day on Saul was jealous of David.*

The next day an evil spirit from God came over Saul and he raged in his house. David was in attendance, playing the harp as at other times, while Saul was holding his spear. Saul poised the spear, thinking to nail David to the wall, but twice David escaped him. Saul then began to fear David, because the LORD was with him, but had departed from Saul himself. Accordingly, Saul removed him from his presence by appointing him a field officer. So David led the people on their military expeditions, and prospered in all his enterprises, for the LORD was with him (1 Samuel 18:6-15).

From that time on, Saul was a successful military commander because David led the military expeditions. Saul however spent the rest of his life trying to kill David. He did not want his servant to take his place as king. The Lord God had already revealed to Saul that David would become king and his descendants would rule over the kingdom of Israel. There were times when David had the opportunity to kill Saul, but David saw this as a great sin that he should not commit. Each time David spared Saul's life, Saul admitted that he was wrong and even showed remorse. This remorse did not last long and Saul always became obstinate as the Pharaoh did each time the Lord had inflicted Egypt with the plagues.

During his forty-year reign as King, Saul gave in to three temptations. Each time he sinned rather than obey God, and the consequences were devastating. He followed the patterns of sin that Israel committed during their forty years in the desert. He disobeyed God by offering the sacrifice. He broke the Law, which states that only the priests of God could offer the sacrifice. The kingdom was taken away from Saul and his descendants after only seven days as Israel's commander.

The gift of prophecy was taken from Saul when he disobeyed the directive against Amalek. The Spirit of God left him, and God no longer spoke to him. At this time it was revealed to Saul that David would be the one that would take his place. Saul could no longer function as a prophet because he would not obey the Word of God as pronounced by the prophet Samuel.

The final temptation came at the end of the forty years when Saul went to a witch to conjure a ghost for him. He asked her to contact Samuel for him, with hopes that Samuel would tell him what he must do. The sin of divination caused him to lose his place as priest of his family. He was not a ministerial priest as the descendants of Aaron, but he was a priest as husband and father in a kingdom of priests. It was revealed to him that his sons would die in battle and he would also die in battle against the Philistines. Saul died the next day and as a result of his sin the position of priest was lost from his family lineage.

These things were summed up in 1 Samuel, 28: 15-19: *Samuel then said to Saul, "Why do you disturb me by conjuring me up?" Saul replied: "I am in great straits, for the Philistines are waging war against me and God has abandoned me. Since he no longer answers me through prophets or in dreams, I have called you to tell me what I should do." To this Samuel said: "But why do you ask me, if the LORD has abandoned you and is with your neighbor? The LORD has done to you what he foretold through me: he has torn the kingdom from your grasp and has given it to your neighbor David.*

"Because you disobeyed the LORD'S directive and would not carry out his fierce anger against Amalek, The LORD has done this to you today. Moreover, the LORD will deliver Israel, and you as well, into the clutches of the Philistines. By tomorrow you and your sons will be with me, and the LORD will have delivered the army of Israel into the hands of the Philistines."

Three Signs

Seven Signs

The Sacrifice

The Gospel According to John

The Jews and Romans Pursued Jesus

Crossed Over

Three-Day Journey

Forty Days

THREE

† Jesus Christ

JESUS REFERRED TO MOSES AS the greatest prophet of Israel, up until John the Baptist, whom Jesus called the greatest prophet born of a woman. Moses was a prophet, priest, and judge, but he was not a king. No one held the offices of priest, prophet, and king simultaneously since Adam. All priests are prophets, and a king may also be a prophet, but no one held the ministerial offices of all three. During the time when the high priest began to function as king, Israel did not have a prophet. There was not a prophet in the land until John the Baptist. At this time, the drought ended because Elijah had appeared to end it. As we recall in Scripture, *Elijah the Tishbite, from Tishbe in Gilead, said to Ahab: "As the LORD, the God of Israel, lives, whom I serve, during these years there shall be no dew or rain except at my word"* (1 Kings 17:1). John the Baptist came to fulfill the prophecy, but he was not the reason for the end of the drought. John came as a sign that the drought will end and that Elijah must come before the Messiah.

Jesus Christ, the Savior of the world came after John appeared and the drought ended. The drought was over because God had manifested himself to the world through him. The good news is that the famine is over and we are saved from death. Now one man, Jesus, holds the office of priest, prophet, and king simultaneously because he is the second Adam.

Jesus is also Judge and Savior. He is a different type of savior than the judges who ruled before the period of the kings. These judges were military commanders and they were prophets. As military commanders, they were saviors, but they were not kings because God was their king.

The Israelites struggled with their temptations in the desert. Because of their lack of faith, it was difficult for them to believe the Word of God. Because of jealousy, it was difficult for them to follow the prophet Moses. Their unwillingness to follow Moses distracted them from their true call to be prophets. By rejecting Moses, they rejected God, and because they refused to live by every word that proceeded from the mouth of God, they lived on bread alone. For forty years, they lived on manna they collected daily.

In the process of restoring order and taking back his plunder, Jesus remained in the desert for forty days and forty nights to fast and to be tempted by the devil. When the devil tempted him to turn the stones into bread, Jesus replied, *"It is written: One does not live by bread alone, but by every word that comes forth from the mouth of God"* (Matthew 4:4). Jesus revealed to us that he is the prophet like Moses whom God had promised to send. Again, the Word of God came to Israel.

God himself was their Savior as when they were set free from slavery in Egypt. Jesus; the Word of God, came down from heaven and he referred to himself as the Bread from Heaven. God himself became flesh in the Incarnation, making Jesus the Word of God and the Prophet. Having a physical body gives him a voice that speaks the invisible word. He makes himself audible and visible.

The Israelites were a priestly people, because God dwelt in their midst. However they tempted God saying, *"Is the LORD in our midst or not?"* (Exodus 17:7). This priestly people also tempted the high priest Aaron when Moses was on the mountain with God for 40 days and 40 nights. God had given him the stone tablets with the commandments, all instructions concerning worship, and the plans for the tabernacle. By the time Moses came down from the mountain, the people had tempted Aaron to make the golden calf. God gave Moses specific instructions in the Law about how they were to worship him, who would be his priest, and how these priests were to offer sacrifices.

The golden calf represents a challenge between the people and God in the sense that the people prefer to make up their own way of worshiping. When Aaron the high priest gave in to their request, he threw himself from the top of the temple. The temple was the body, which consisted of the priestly people, and Aaron was the head because he was the high priest. What Aaron experienced was similar to what the first man Adam experienced when he ate the forbidden fruit. He listened to his wife and disobeyed God. Aaron listened to the people and disobeyed God.

The devil tempted Jesus a second time. *The devil took him to the holy city, and made him stand on the parapet of the temple, and said to him, "If you are the Son of God, throw yourself down. For it is written: 'He will command his angels concerning you,' and 'with their hands they will support you, lest you dash your foot against a stone.' " Jesus answered him, "Again it is written, 'You shall not put the LORD your God, to the test.'"* (Matthew 4:6-7). Jesus is the High Priest and he refused to throw himself down from the top of the Temple as Aaron did. Jesus was restoring order and revealed in this way that the head should not follow the body, and more importantly that the Creator should not be tempted to follow a creature.

The third temptation that the Israelites faced was to worship the foreign gods of the other kingdoms. To worship foreign gods is to violate the first commandment. This commandment must be important since it is first. The Lord called Israel a royal priesthood and a kingdom of priests. If they remained loyal to the Lord they would eventually rule over other nations. If they worshiped false gods, then they would become slaves. They would become slaves to sin and slaves to the other kingdoms. All of this came into fulfillment as the Lord had forewarned. They had become slaves to sin and slaves to other kingdoms. Instead of possessing the land, they themselves had become possessed. God himself would have to come down from heaven and free them as he did for their ancestors in Egypt.

Jesus experienced a similar temptation. *Then the devil took him up to a very high mountain, and showed him all the kingdoms of the world in their magnificence, and he said to* him, *"All these I shall give to you, if you will prostrate yourself and worship me." At this, Jesus said to him, "Get away, Satan! It is written: 'The Lord, your God, shall you worship and him alone shall you serve.' "Then the devil left him and behold angels came and ministered to him* (Matthew 4:8-11).

What Jesus had accomplished was that he bound the devil. The devil bound Adam and plundered his house. Now the devil attempted to bind Jesus, because he knew that Jesus came as the new Adam. Jesus is the strong man and the devil could not bind him. Jesus did not sin and bound the devil instead. Then Jesus began to take back his plunder. He went into a synagogue and cast a demon out of a person. He gave sight to the blind, hearing to the deaf, and healing to the sick.

Jesus united the offices of priest, prophet, and king once again. Everyone who is baptized enters into Jesus' office as priest, prophet, and king. God calls everyone to accept Jesus as Savior. The holy Catholic Church sends her ministers to sanctify, teach, and govern. These ministers she ordains as priests to serve the royal priesthood of the baptized.

I have spoken about Jesus being the second Adam and reuniting the offices of priest, prophet, and king, but what about being savior and judge? I will explain how we can understand Jesus also as savior and judge. Let's begin with Jesus' baptism by John the Baptist in the Jordan.

†

THREE SIGNS

The baptism of Jesus by John the Baptist marks the beginning of Jesus' public ministry. The Gospel according to John has Jesus' manifestation at the wedding feast at Cana when he turned water into wine. When compared to the first chapter of this book where Israel was brought out of slavery, the first three signs or miracles established that there is only one God, and only he can give life. Although Moses and Aaron performed miracles, it was actually God who had accomplished these things. The third sign, when life was brought forth from the dust, signified that God is the Creator of all things, especially life.

When Saul was anointed king, the third sign revealed that it was the Spirit of the Lord that caused the guild of prophets to enter a prophetic state. The Spirit of God changed Saul into a different man, as Samuel had prophesied. While Samuel may have been the instrument, it was actually God who anointed Saul as King of Israel.

Similarly, John baptized Jesus in the Jordan, but it was God who anointed Jesus with the Holy Spirit. This time the sign revealed another great mystery, the mystery of sacraments. John was minister and he used the element of water. The form consisted of the words he used when baptizing Jesus. As minister, John stood in the place of God the Father. *And a voice came from the heavens, saying, "This is my beloved Son, with whom I am well pleased"* (Matthew 3:17). John the

Baptist revealed what happened in the spiritual world; that which is normally hidden from the naked eyes and the ears of mortals. What John did was efficacious and fulfilled all righteousness, as Jesus explained. John caused an effect to happen in the spiritual world. The Catechism of the Catholic Church, Paragraph 1228 – II: Baptism in the Church, summarizes what happens during the sacrament of baptism in this way, *Hence Baptism is a bath of water in which the "imperishable seed" of the Word of God produces its life-giving effect.*[32] St. Augustine says of Baptism: *"The word is brought to the material element, and it becomes a sacrament."*[33] This definition explains that Jesus' baptism in the Jordan is the institution of this sacrament. The Word of God was brought to the material element of water.

These three signs occur differently in the Gospel of Matthew than in the Gospel of John. The Baptism of Jesus as recorded in the Gospel of Matthew gives a detailed account of what happened to Jesus. The Gospel according to John reveals what happens to us because of Jesus' baptism. Matthew's gospel provides a clear demonstration of the things necessary for a sacrament. One interpretation would be that, in Matthew, the King was anointed; in the gospel of John, the firstborn Son is also Savior to his siblings.

There are parallels between *the heavens were opened [for him], and he saw the Spirit of God descending like a dove [and] coming upon him* (Matthew 3:16) and *"The true light, which enlightens everyone, was coming into the world"* (John 1:9).

God the Father spoke from the heavens and acknowledged his Son: *"This is my beloved Son, with whom I am well pleased"* (Matthew 3:17). Compare this to *"But to those who did accept him he gave power to become children of God, to those who believe in his name, who were born not by natural generation nor by human choice nor by a man's decision but of God"* (John 1:12).

The third sign is in Matthew 4:1: *Then Jesus was led by the Spirit into the desert to be tempted by the devil.* This event parallels John 1:14: *And the Word became flesh and made his dwelling among us, and we saw his glory as of the Father's only Son, full of grace and truth.*

The threefold signs reveal Jesus also as high priest. He is High Priest of all those who are baptized in comparison to the first Adam being high priest to all those who are born of natural reproduction. Jesus is High Priest and he gives his Spirit in baptism, the true light, which enlightens everyone. By the words of the minister, we become children of God, and the Word of God makes his dwelling among us.

The illustration below may help visualize the relationship between these Scripture passages.

MATTHEW	JOHN
3:16 After Jesus was baptized, he came up from the water and behold, the heavens were opened (for him), and he saw the Spirit of God descending like a dove, (and) coming upon him.	1:5 the true light, which enlightens everyone, was coming into the world.
3:17 and a voice came from the heavens, saying, "This is my beloved Son, with whom I am well pleased."	1:12 But to those who did accept him he gave power to become children of God, to those who believe in his name,
4:1-2 Then Jesus was led by the Spirit into the desert to be tempted by the devil. He fasted for forty days and forty nights, and afterwards he was hungry.	1:14 And the word became flesh and made his dwelling among us, and we saw his glory, the glory as of the Father's only Son, full of grace and truth.

All three signs clearly demonstrate it was God the Father who anointed Jesus. The third sign reveals the Incarnation, which is something that only God could accomplish. The Word became flesh and dwelt among us is that definitive point in history in which the beginning, the end, and the center are manifested in time. God himself, who exists outside of time, has entered time and space to make his dwelling among us and in this way lead us out of slavery and the darkness of sin. He is the Alpha and the Omega, yet, in the Incarnation, he is also the center of time. He is the God who was, who is, and who will be.

The first two signs were instants in time because only those who saw the dove and heard the voice experienced the signs, regardless of how eternal the effects. However, the third sign in which Jesus was led into the desert to dwell for 40 days and 40 nights parallels the Incarnation. The Incarnation itself is not merely a moment in time, but an eternal reality, which exists in real time. The baptism of Jesus was a sign that Jesus is the Son of Man because he was born of a woman and entered humanity to dwell among the descendants of Adam. It is important that we acknowledge Jesus as the Son of God and the Son of Man.

†

SEVEN SIGNS

The three signs in the first chapter of John are very encouraging. The true light has come to enlighten us. We can become children of God, and God has come to make his dwelling among us. It is as Jesus calls it, the good news.

After the three signs hidden within the Baptism of Jesus, came the seven signs. The seven signs recorded in the Gospel according to John are different from the seven plagues in Egypt. They are also different from the seven days that King Saul was fighting against the Philistines. The seven signs John writes about reveal the goodness of God pointedly and directly. We who love God know that God is love. We know that God is truth and all good.

It is more difficult to recognize the goodness of God

where he showed forth his power in the plagues against the Egyptians. The Lord was saving his people from slavery and freeing them from the hardships and oppression they suffered in Egypt. This was a good thing for the Israelites, but what did it mean for the Egyptians? Actually, it gave the Egyptians a chance to come to know the true God. It gave them an opportunity to enter a relationship with the God of Abraham, Isaac, and Jacob. The memory of these events was marked on the minds of the Egyptians and in their history. It was clearly proven that the gods of Egypt did not exist. The plagues in Egypt were for the purpose of setting the Israelites free, but also to allow the Egyptians to see the power of God, that they may be brought into God's plan of salvation. The plagues were for a good purpose.

The same reasoning may be applied to understanding the seven days that King Saul fought against the Philistines immediately after he was anointed King of Israel. The Israelites wanted a king to protect them. It was only proper that the truth be revealed to them. The truth would make them free, and the truth was that their newly anointed king could not protect them the way God protected them. With God as their King, every enemy of Israel was powerless. Israel rejected God and elected to have a man rule over them. The Philistines overpowered the Israelites and Saul's only hope was to survive for seven days until Samuel came to offer the holocaust and peace offerings for him.

The effects of the seven plagues were menacing and disastrous to the Egyptians. For King Saul, the first three signs were a great blessing, but the seven days were disastrous. The stressful circumstances Saul and his military faced were from the hands of the Philistines.

When humanity encounters God in the Incarnation things are quite different. In the Incarnation, the three signs are a great blessing to everyone, as are the seven signs. This is quite a contrast from the story of the Egyptians in which all 10 plagues brought sorrow to the Egyptians. The good news is that God sent his Son Jesus for the salvation of all humanity. During the story of the Israelites leaving Egypt, the focus was on God saving the Israelites, which is good news. However, the plagues meant also that God had come to pass judgment on the gods of Egypt.

Note the chart below, which compares the 10 plagues in Egypt with the signs given in the life of King Saul and the signs given in the Gospel of John.

EGYPTIANS	SAUL	JESUS
All 10 plagues are Disastrous	3 signs are blessings 7 days are disastrous	All 10 signs are blessings
Water Turned into Blood	Met two men near Rachel's tomb – the asses have been found	Jesus was baptized and the Holy Spirit descended upon him in the form of a dove.
The Frogs	Met three men going up to God at Bethel – offered him two wave offerings of bread	The voice from heaven said, "This is my beloved Son."
The Gnats	Met a band of prophets in a prophetic state – the Spirit of God rushed upon him	The Spirit led him into the desert to be tempted.
The Flies	Day 1 – In danger of death	The Wedding at Cana
The Pestilence	Day 2 – In danger of death	Second Sign at Cana
The Boils	Day 3 – In danger of death	Cure on a Sabbath

The Hail	Day 4 – In danger of death	Multiplication of the Loaves
The Locust	Day 5 – In danger of death	Walking on the Water
The Darkness	Day 6 – In danger of death	The Man Born Blind
The Death of the First-born	Day 7 – In danger of death	The Raising of Lazarus

God desires what is good for his people. He sent his Son Jesus to lead us out of the darkness of sin and death. Every good father wants to pour out blessings upon his children. The seven signs in the gospel of John are blessings from our Holy Father. It is a demonstration confirming what Jesus said, "I desire that you have life and have it more abundantly." We may look at these signs as blessings. They occurred in that precise time in history, perfectly structured to accomplish a desired end. Here are examples of how each sign was a blessing.

1. The gift of the Holy Spirit is the beginning of life. We now have the Spirit of God living and dwelling in our midst. He is the Lord and the giver of life. Jesus changed the water to wine as the beginning of his signs in Cana in Galilee and so revealed his glory.

2. The royal official asked Jesus to heal his son for the same reasons that God does not want any of his children to perish. Jesus healed the boy who was near death.

3. Some illnesses we can live with, but they limit our ability to have life more abundantly. Whether the person is ill, blind, lame, or crippled, it is not the life that we were created for. We are the children of the Almighty God, the God who is perfect in all his ways. Jesus healed the man at the sheep gate. This man had been ill for thirty-eight years, and now he was able to take up his mat and walk. The man was reminded by Jesus, *"Look, you are well; do not sin anymore, so that nothing worse may happen to you"* (John 5:14).

4. When our sins have been forgiven, we are allowed to eat from the table of the Lord. This food strengthens us for

the journey. Jesus fed the multitude for this reason; he did not want to send them away hungry for fear they may collapse on the way. We call the Eucharist the Great Sacrament, because it is the body and blood of Jesus.

5. The church does not have to worry about the floodwaters. Strong winds and high waves are no threat to the church because Jesus is able to walk on water and lead the church to her destination.

6. Everyone who inherits the original sin is born blind. The sixth sign was when Jesus sent a man blind from birth to wash in the Pool of Siloam. Likewise, we are sent to the church to be healed from our blindness and given sight. The Pharisees did not believe that they were blind and Jesus' response was, "your sin remains." The reality is our eyes are open because we are descendants of Adam and Eve. We must first become blind before we are given sight. Jesus made clay and put over the eyes of the blind man, but he did not receive his sight until he went to the pool and washed.

7. Jesus raised Lazarus from the dead. This is the last sign. Everyone will be resurrected from the dead on judgment day. Some will come out as Lazarus did to hear the words that will sound like sweet music "Untie him and let him go."

Every one of these signs reveal Jesus came down from heaven not only for our salvation, but also to pour out the blessings of God upon us. He desires that we have life and have it more abundantly. The good news is that the kingdom of heaven is at hand. All that is required of us is to repent from our sinful ways and to accept salvation from God. We should accept Jesus for who he is, the only begotten Son of God.

In recognizing that everything Jesus did was for our benefit, the questions arise as to why was Jesus rejected and why did his opponents put up so much resistance? When rejection and resistance proved ineffective, Jesus' opponents resorted to persecution. When persecution did not silence Jesus, his enemies decided to put him to death. Even so, death was not enough to satisfy their anger and hostility. Jesus had to suffer a type of death that would discourage others from following him. Why so much determination to stop someone who does good and good only?

While the answer is not simple, there are principles that remain constant throughout time. As in the story of the Israelites and their battles with the Egyptians for freedom, God passed judgment on the gods of Egypt. God did not say that he came to pass judgment on the people of Egypt, because in his goodness he desires that all will be saved.

During the time King Saul was Israel's military commander, he fought many nations, but the true enemies of God were the false gods and not the people. This fundamental principle also exists in the story we are now viewing. With the seven signs, Jesus provides for the needs of people. The first sign revealed that we are forever trying to make ends meet. Except for the wealthy, many people are like the couple at the wedding feast hoping to have enough resources to accomplish even the simplest things in life. In most cases, that resource is money. Yet we know that *the love of money is the root of all evil* (1 Timothy 6:10). Jesus healed the sick, and raised Lazarus from the dead. Both sickness and death came into the world because of sin. Whoever is the author of death is the cause of all suffering, and of all oppression and slavery. Jesus explained that it is the devil that is responsible for these evils. He spoke these words to those trying to kill him, "*You belong to your father the devil and you willingly carry out your father's desires. He was a murderer from the beginning and does not stand in truth, because there is no truth in him. When he tells a lie, he speaks in character, because he is a liar and the father of lies*" (John 8:44). He is the accuser who goes to God and accuses us. For this reason, God sent to us the Advocate who speaks to God for us. So, the fundamental principle is a way of understanding whom the true enemies of God are. Jesus began to remove these enemies, known as unclean spirits, from those who were possessed. He also freed people from oppression and obsession.

The real tragedy is that sometimes we cannot differentiate between who is responsible for good and who is responsible for evil. As long as we persist in self-will the devil appears to be good and benevolent to us. He appears to be a liberator and one who understands our needs and desires. We are trapped into thinking that the one who allows us to sin without experiencing guilt is the one who loves us. That is because the devil convinces us that we have not sinned when actually we have. This is the great deception of the devil and his angels. They love no one, and the devil will convict the very people that he liberated from the ways of God. He will go to God and say "Look at the sins they have committed." On top of all of this he will make us feel guilty about the sins he tempted us to commit with the idea that we cannot be forgiven.

It is easy to say that God is responsible for good and the devil is responsible for evil, but how do we distinguish who is who among the unseen? When God does something good for us and we call it evil, there is definitely a warped perception of reality among men. And the battle among those humans who opposed Jesus would have arisen because they perceived the good works of Jesus as a means of deception. It must be that they trust Jesus no more than Adam and Eve trusted God once the devil convinced them that God was deceiving them. Jesus came to reconcile us with God and he proved that God cannot deceive nor can he be deceived. This is something proven in his passion, death, and resurrection.

On Palm Sunday, the Israelites accepted Jesus as their Savior and King. Once again, Israel had God as her King. God came as a mighty warrior and began to save his people by cleansing the temple. He came as the Prince of Peace. The peace that he brought was unity, and it means that he freed them from everything that divides. He did so because his enemy the devil seeks to scatter, slaughter, and devour. It did not take long before Israel was ready to rid herself from the yoke of her new King. Was the yoke heavy? It was only heavy for those who were not willing to repent. Israel had rejected God once again as her King, and on Holy Thursday Jesus offered a sacrifice so that death would pass over his firstborn.

†

THE SACRIFICE

What makes this night different? The answer to this question would be explained to the children of Israel from one generation to the next. They were reminded of how their ancestors were slaves in Egypt and at Passover how they ate their meal with their staff in hand with no time to let the bread rise. On the night of the first Passover, the blood of the lambs on the doors prevented the angel of death from killing the firstborn of Israel. The Israelites celebrated Passover every year from that time on to commemorate what happened on the night of the Passover in Egypt.

Jesus commemorated the Eucharist as the first Passover for the Christian people. *"I have eagerly desired to eat this Passover with you before I suffer"* (Luke 22:15). This statement has great significance for the Christian people. Passover was important for Jesus and his disciples because it marked the beginning of Jesus' exodus from his life on earth. Jesus revealed that he is the Passover Lamb and his blood would protect the apostles because they are his firstborn. They would be protected from the angel of death who would come in the middle of the night. One apostle did not heed to the warning of the Word of God and he went outside of the house. That person was Judas Iscariot. He tried to offer a different sacrifice. Judas sacrifice was not acceptable to God, nor was his sacrifice of repentance and the return of the money acceptable to the leaders in Jerusalem. In the middle of the night, which was the time that the Angel of death came, Judas Iscariot hung himself. Jesus did not lose any of those whom his Father gave him because they remained in the house protected by Jesus' blood. The apostles are the firstborn of the new Israel, but Judas Iscariot, whom Jesus called the son of perdition, went out as the firstborn of Egypt.

Judas Iscariot was the twelfth apostle, as Benjamin was the twelfth son of Jacob. King Saul was also from the tribe of Benjamin. Saul offered the unacceptable sacrifice because the Law forbade what he did. What Judas Iscariot did was forbidden, because Satan entered him and he tried to offer himself. Jesus called Judas to follow him, but Judas instead went before Jesus. When Satan entered Judas Iscariot, he became a so-called deity, the son of perdition. Judas now takes action as Pharaoh did. Pharaoh considered himself a deity, the descendant of their chief god. Of course, Satan's sacrifice is unacceptable even if Judas repented and died immediately afterwards. His actions cannot be compared to Jesus who was conceived without sin and committed no sins his entire life. Jesus is the acceptable sacrifice to God the Father. He is the Lamb without stain or blemish, and Christians understand the crucifixion to be the work of God.

The understanding of the acceptable sacrifice for the Christian people must come from our understanding of Judaism. God revealed himself to the Israelites and in the Law he revealed how he intended to be worshiped. We believe Jesus fulfilled the Law and we received the promise of God, which is the Holy Spirit. Christians accept Jesus' sacrifice on Calvary as our means of salvation. For the Catholic Christian, the last Passover that Jesus celebrated with his disciples was the beginning of a new way of worshiping. God himself came down from heaven and changed the way that we worship.

When Israel received the Law, Moses sprinkled the blood on their heads as a sign that the covenant was ratified by their acceptance of the Law. The Israelites were forbidden to consume blood even when eating meats. At the Last Supper, God changed the worship; this time to ratify the covenant the apostles had to drink the blood. It is a new covenant in which the objective is to keep the person's conscience clean. The covenant is internal and we drink the blood. This is in strong contrast with the old covenant, which was external; its objective was to keep the person's flesh clean and thus avoid defiling the Temple when the person entered.

We continue to celebrate Jesus' Passover because it was the first Passover for the church, the new Israel. Jews continue to celebrate Passover, and their Passover is as valid today as it was the night of the first Passover in Egypt. It is valid because Almighty God gave it to them. The Passover that the Jews celebrate did not come from the imagination of men. God gave specific instructions about how they were to celebrate this great mystery. They were responsible to continue to celebrate this mystery and only God himself could change their worship.

Christians differ however because we believe that Jesus is the Messiah. We believe that God could and did become a man. Why do we believe this to be true? First, we believe it by faith, but also in the great mystery of Jesus' baptism we believe as written in the Scriptures, *"and he saw the Spirit of*

God descending like a dove and coming upon him" (Matthew 3:16-17). We believe that a voice came from the heavens and said, *"This is my beloved Son, with whom I am well pleased."* And we believe that the Holy Spirit led Jesus into the desert to fast for 40 days and 40 nights, and to be tempted by the devil. The three signs in the first chapter of the Gospel of John also unfolded part of this great mystery. Jesus' baptism was not for his sake but for the sake of all humanity. The Holy Spirit descended from heaven to enlighten us, because he is the true light. We who accept Jesus become children of God. And when we become children of God, he makes his dwelling among us.

Holy Thursday for us is the first Passover. It is the first Eucharistic celebration in which Jesus offers himself as thanksgiving to his Father, his God, and our God. The parallels to Egypt are strong because we have a Passover lamb and specific instructions on how to continue this first Passover. Jesus said, *"Do this in remembrance of me."* This way it is passed from generation to generation in a similar fashion as the Israelites explaining to their children why this night is different. Our beliefs are different from Israel's because we believe that Jesus is the Word of God, the High Priest, and our King. Thus, he fulfilled the role of Moses the prophet, Aaron the high priest, and God our King and Savior. He fulfills the role of Joshua the military commander. He is the Passover lamb and he is the new Israel.

When Jesus saved his firstborn on Holy Thursday, he also began his exodus out of Egypt. The leaders of the Jews refused to let the people go and attempted to keep them enslaved to the Law. But Jesus desired to set them free and gave them the promise that God made to Abraham. Jesus prayed that we might be one as he and his Father are one. This can only be accomplished when we have the same Spirit dwelling within us. That Spirit is the Holy Spirit, the Spirit of Truth.

God also revealed all things evil that work against the salvation of humanity. All of these things God revealed as the image of Satan, and he revealed this in the person of Judas Iscariot. Judas personifies all those working against God and his plan of salvation for man. Because Judas was the twelfth apostle symbolizing the tribe of Benjamin, he symbolized Judaism in its present state at that time. He personifies Annas the high priest compared to Moses the prophet, and Caiaphas the high priest compared to Aaron. Judas also personifies Herod the king compared to Joshua. Judas confessed his sin and gave up his life in suicide, which contradicts the Word of God. In this way, he personifies also a perversion of the meaning of true sacrifice. His sacrifice mocks the perfect sacrifice of Jesus. And last and possibly most importantly, Satan entered Judas. This appears to be Satan's last attempt to become flesh and to offer the son of perdition in the middle of the night as compared to Jesus who will take on the sins of the world in the middle of the day on Good Friday. These images personified in Judas Iscariot are horrible and most unpleasant.

No matter how unpleasant it is to think of, Satan did enter him and this great perversion mocked the Incarnation of Jesus Christ where the Spirit of God overshadowed the Blessed Virgin Mary. The Spirit of God entered a person and God himself became man. Satan's attempt to take on flesh gives evidence he is trying to save humanity from the Lord God as he did in the Garden of Eden with Adam and Eve. This is also why Judas Iscariot most likely was called the thief. He held the moneybag and used to steal from it, so literally, he was a thief. Judas also acted as a guide for those who came for Jesus with lanterns, torches, swords, and clubs. So, in a hidden mystery Judas Iscariot came as the thief in the night.

Jesus said, *"Follow me"* to his apostles and all who desired to be his disciples. Judas Iscariot however rejected Jesus and went before him to offer sacrifice. The sacrifice and the priest who offered it was rejected just like the firstborn who died in Egypt the night of the first Passover. Judas' sacrifice was rejected as much as King Saul's sacrifice was rejected. The kingdom was taken away from Saul and his descendants, and the priesthood was taken away from Pharaoh and the firstborn of Egypt. *Jesus said, "All who came before me are thieves and robbers, but the sheep did not listen to them"* (John 10:8). This statement is partially fulfilled in the person of Judas Iscariot. Judas personifies all those who rejected Jesus whether prophet, priest, king, or the angel that led them into rebellion.

Jesus offered his life at the Last Supper and death passed over his firstborn; it was the beginning of the feast of unleavened bread. During his exodus, he was chased down as the Pharaoh pursued the Israelites into the Red Sea. At this time, Jesus saved his military in the same way that God saved Israel. God saved his military from death in the Red Sea and from the Egyptian army. Jesus is the revelation of the All Holy God, the God who is Love and Truth. Jesus alone was necessary for the salvation of the firstborn. Judas Iscariot personified all that is evil and worked against the salvation of the firstborn. John the beloved disciple of Jesus at the foot of the cross personified Jesus' military. I will attempt to explain this further in the next chapter.

†

THE JEWS AND ROMANS PURSUED JESUS

At the Last Supper, Jesus is the High Priest and he offered himself as the sacrifice for our salvation. He also ordained his apostles as priests and told them to continue to offer the bread and wine as the memorial of his suffering and death. We have a new high priest and a new sacrifice. None of Jesus' firstborn were harmed except the son of perdition, that the Scripture might be fulfilled. With Jesus as the new High Priest and his apostles ordained as his firstborn, they were brought into direct conflict with the old order. The priests who were descendants of Aaron condemned Jesus.

The servant was replacing the priesthood from the tribe of Levi. Jesus came to serve and not to be served. These are his words. Since Jesus at this time was being glorified, he was replacing the high priest Aaron with himself, and the descendants of Aaron he replaced with his sons, the apostles. The descendants of the apostles, those ordained in the future would be the priesthood of the future. Jesus and the bread and wine were replacing the Levite priesthood and the sacrifice of animals. The high priest and all the Sadducees did not take this lightly and they fought to hold their place of honor as much as Pharaoh and the Egyptians fought to hold their place. Yet again, the servant has replaced the oppressors.

I would like to explain what I meant when referring to St. John the Beloved as one who personifies Jesus' military. The ten plagues revealed Moses as prophet. He was as God to Pharaoh, and Aaron was Moses' prophet. The night of the Passover revealed more about the priesthood. Aaron was the first priest, and is father of all firstborn in the priesthood. Jesus is the Word of God and he is the Prophet as was Moses, although greater than Moses. During Jesus' public ministry he spoke what is true and many people accepted him as a great prophet. In the 10 signs as Prophet, he blessed people in many ways. At the Last Supper, Jesus spoke as the priest presiding over a liturgy. He saved the priesthood, his firstborn.

Things changed the next day during the crucifixion because now it was the military that fought against Jesus. They oppose Jesus as King of the Jews and, of course, the Romans had Caesar as their king. Jesus the Servant was being glorified as King. The New Israel will have God as their King as when Israel crossed the Red Sea. This was a new creation with Jesus being the light to show everyone the way to life. He labored during the crucifixion in order that all his disciples may share the breath of life, his Holy Spirit. The military that fought against Jesus consisted of the people of God, and the Roman government. It was the image of church members and the state uniting their efforts to be set free from God. The Jewish leaders handed Jesus over to Pontius Pilate, requesting that Jesus be crucified. Within the story of the pursuit to bring

Jesus back as a servant, the oppressors preferred that Jesus die a cruel death rather than to be glorified as King and rule in their place. The oppressors are no different from Pharaoh or King Saul.

As mentioned earlier Jesus is Prophet, Priest, and King. More importantly, he is God and he is forming a new creation. Jesus had already accomplished his works of salvation during his public ministry as the Word of God, meaning as Prophet and Priest. During the crucifixion it appears that he completed the work he began on Palm Sunday when he entered Jerusalem as King.

Jesus on the cross took on the sins of the world. It was his time to enter the Red Sea. For Jesus to bear our sins on the cross he had to, as the Son of David, march in the Philistine Army. In the meantime, those who were taunting him told him to come down from the cross. *"Aha! You would destroy the temple and rebuild it in three days, save yourself by coming down from the cross"* (Mark 15:29-30). Jesus could not come down from the cross without committing a sin. It was the will of his Father that he suffer this way and die for our sins. But those who tempted Jesus to come down from the cross would like to bring him back as a servant.

Because Jesus emptied himself and took the form of a slave when he became man, it was difficult for the world to see him exalted and glorified as the King of Kings. It was also difficult for them to see him as God dwelling among men. So, *"Come down from the cross,"* was the battle cry of those who would like to bring him back into servitude. As the Egyptians who followed the Israelites into the Red Sea, they are saying,

"Come back and serve us. If you are not willing to serve us, we will kill you." The services that Jesus rendered had ended: healing the sick, giving sight to the blind, hearing to the deaf, casting demons out of people, and freeing them from the torment of demons as David did when he played the harp for Saul. These people preferred that Jesus died. They were not much different from the Egyptians or King Saul.

When Jesus took on the sins of the world, he did not try to come back from the Red Sea into Egypt. It means that he was willing to trust God his Father and go forward through the Red Sea. He was willing to march with the Philistine army even when they were going to battle against Israel. David knew that if Saul were killed in this battle, David himself would have been responsible for the death of God's anointed. God provided a way out for David, and David did not have to sin to accomplish the will of God. When Jesus trusted his Father with his life he said, *"Father, forgive them, they know not what they do"* Jesus replied to the criminal on his right, *"Amen, I say to you, today you will be with me in Paradise." It was now about noon and darkness came over the whole land until three in the afternoon because of an eclipse of the sun* (Luke 23:34, 43-45).

Does anyone think that Jesus himself was in darkness? I think not, because Jesus is the light and although he had taken on the sins of the world, the darkness could not overcome the light. Those who were pursuing Jesus were in darkness, but Jesus marched forward in the light as the Israelites marched through the Red Sea in the light. Those who saw Jesus as an enemy and wished for his death even tried to bring on his death by tempting him to come down from the cross and commit a grave sin.

Jesus' enemies could not pursue him in the darkness, because they could not see him. They could not see Jesus, just as the Egyptians could not see Israel in the Red Sea. Once Jesus came through the darkness of sin, at three o'clock the eclipse of the sun had ended. The light returned to the world as the morning when Israel crossed the Red Sea. At this point, they saw the Egyptians lying dead on the shore, but God's army came through unharmed. St. John, the beloved disciple of Jesus, personifies the army of the new Israel. God chose to reveal in John the beloved disciple, Jesus' military. John is normally listed as the fourth apostle compared to Judah, being the fourth son of Jacob. Sometimes in the Gospel he is referred to as the third apostle, symbolic of Levi. He is a priest king, and he represents the people of God who are a kingdom of priests. He took Jesus' mother into his home, because she is the Ark of the Covenant, and the Ark of the Covenant belongs in the Temple in Judah.

CROSSED OVER

Did Jesus cross over into the spiritual realm during the three hours of darkness on the cross? Was this the battle between the Kingdom of Light and the kingdom of darkness? Jesus did not have the same veil of the flesh to separate him from the spiritual world as we do. However, he was separated in the sense that he did not inherit the original sin nor did he ever commit a sin. So when Jesus took on the sins of the world he crossed over into the spiritual realm to a place that he had never been. He entered the abode of the dead and had to pass through this valley of darkness. He had no fear of the darkness since he himself is the light. This means that Jesus was never lost; he always knew where he was going. Jesus is the light that entered the darkness and the darkness did not overcome the light.

The three hours of darkness on the cross was a battle between God who is light and Satan who is the ruler of the kingdom of darkness. The people that oppose Jesus mainly consist of slaves who are deceived, oppressors who are oppressed themselves but do not know it, and religious and political leaders who cooperate with evil. These people pursued Jesus until he entered the three hours of darkness. Once Jesus entered the darkness by taking on our sins, darkness came over the world and those who were pursuing him could not see him, but Jesus has light the whole time and he knows where he is headed because he is the Light.

Jesus is the Son of David and he treated the Jews the way that David treated King Saul. He treated them as God's chosen people and he would not do anything to harm them. Even when they were trying to kill Jesus, he was more concerned with saving their lives. David would not do anything against God's anointed and he carried his cross as Jesus did to avoid sinning against God. Jesus also gave them relief from the torment of evil spirits. Anyone who came before Jesus possessed and tormented by evil spirits was set free. He would cast the demon out and free that person from the torment in the same way that David would play the harp to soothe Saul from the torments of the evil spirit. Here again God used one person to personify a group. King Saul was relieved from the torment of the evil spirit repeatedly by David playing the harp, whereas Jesus cast demons out of many people.

Something else that King Saul did was to bring back King Agag, the King of Amalek, and the animals that he was commanded to kill. The Lord had put everything in Amalek under a ban. Saul killed all of the people but spared the life of the king. Can this be interpreted as fighting evil by killing all of the evil people but signing a peace treaty with the devil? Because of this disobedience to God, the Spirit of God left Saul, and from that day on the Lord spoke to Saul neither in dreams nor by prophets, and as revealed in Exodus 17:16, *"the LORD will war against Amalek through the centuries."* Jesus appears to have fulfilled this prophecy. When the Jews accepted Jesus as their King on Palm Sunday, he entered Jerusalem, went to the Temple, and cleansed it by casting out those who sold sheep and oxen and doves. He also drove the animals out of the Temple area to let the people know that it is obedience God desires, not sacrifice. He also turned over the tables of the moneychangers. Jesus corrected the error of King Saul as Samuel did when he put the King of Amalek to death. The devil is the ruler of this world and he cannot be put to death, but Jesus showed the ruler of this world has been judged, condemned, and cast out. The animals under the ban were also thrown out and would not be used for sacrifice to the Lord as Saul claimed they should be. When Samuel asked him why did he not slaughter those animals, Saul replied he brought them back to sacrifice to the Lord.

David always did what was good for Saul, yet Saul pursued David to kill him. Saul feared David because he knew that God was with David. He pursued David until David went into the territory of the Philistines. The Jews have treated Jesus the way that Saul treated David and now Jesus will come out of the darkness as David his father did.

At three o'clock in the afternoon God gave those who pursued Jesus a glance, which threw them into confusion. The people pursuing Jesus at three o'clock received a preview of the resurrected Christ. When we come face to face with God on Judgment Day, we realize it is too late to make decisions. That is the confusion that Pharaoh and his army faced, and it was the cause of Saul's distress after hearing his judgment from Samuel. Jesus came out of the darkness of sin without being harmed by sin. He suffered in the flesh from the torture of the crucifixion, but spiritually he was not harmed or even wounded.

Ironically, the people that opposed Jesus assisted him in conquering sin and death. Jesus was judged, condemned, and cast out from the people of God and from the world. Isn't that what Jesus said about Satan when he said that the ruler of this world has been judged, condemned and cast out? Upon leaving the darkness, Jesus united himself with his mother in the way that Israel was baptized into Moses upon crossing the Red Sea. Jesus' mother remained silent in the assembly; perhaps she understood what St. Paul later said in Scripture that she would be saved by bearing children. John took her into his home because he was ordained priest, prophet, and king. He also took her in as his mother, meaning he also represents those who are baptized as priest, prophet, and king. John represents every one of us who become adopted children of God and adopted children of Mary. If John represents God's military that was saved from sin and death after the three hours darkness, it is because he represents the tribe of Judah whom the Lord said would go first and lead the attack. If this is true, then we are the rest of God's military and we were saved from sin and death also. We are responsible to follow John and to continue the attack against the kingdom of darkness.

The three hours of darkness also seemed to foreshadow three days and three nights in the belly of the earth. Some events pointed to the resurrection. The earth quaked and the graves opened, people went home beating their breast. The Roman centurion said, "Surely this man was the Son of God." The angel rolled the stone away from the tomb. Many of the saints who were dead followed Jesus from the abode of the dead; they came out of their graves and appeared to people they knew.

†

THE THREE-DAY JOURNEY

One of the last things that Jesus said before he died on the cross was, *"I thirst."* He was about to begin his three days and nights in the belly of the earth. He was no longer to live in the land of those who live in the flesh, since he had crossed over into the spiritual world. I believe Jesus entered that place where many people thirst. For three days and three nights, Jesus would be their leader as Moses led the Israelites after they crossed the Red Sea.

We know little about the three-day journey in the desert to offer sacrifice, because the Scriptures say little about it. The Israelite experience of being set free from slavery allowed them to go on a three-day journey in the desert to offer sacrifice to God. For Jesus it must have been important, because it was placed between the crucifixion and the resurrection.

Three days in the desert without finding water brought the Israelites to the point of desperation. Their need for water reflects the desire to remain alive. Likewise, when David and his men arrived at Negeb and Ziklag after a three-day journey, the disappointment of finding their families taken captive was devastating. In both circumstances, it was a life and death matter.

When Jesus died on the cross, he also crossed over into the spiritual, and was judged. Jesus faced judgment at the end of his earthly life similar to the Israelites and the Egyptians. David and Saul faced judgment also. The fate of the Egyptians was death, while the Israelites progressed to the next stage of life. Saul and his family faced death, while David and his men were saved from death. The ruler of this world, Satan was judged, condemned and cast out, while Jesus entered the Holy of Holies. Israel and David received mercy from God, but Jesus is without sin. Jesus entered the Holy of Holies as the high priest on the Day of Atonement. On this day, the high priest enters the Holy of Holies three times. When the ritual ended,

God would forgive the high priest of his sin and he would live and come out to the people who are praying and calling to remembrance of their sins. Jesus' role is entirely different from Israel and David's because Jesus is the Savior, he is without sin, and he is God.

Israel was freed from slavery in Egypt, and David was freed from oppression and persecution from Saul. God passed judgment on the gods of Egypt who enslaved the Israelites, and Jesus, the Son of God, took the keys of death from Satan.

I would like to return to the creation story for insights into the Passion of our Lord Jesus. Beginning first with the crucifixion, can we call the sixth day of the week the first day? On the sixth day of creation, God made man in his own image, and Jesus was glorified on the cross. In Jesus' words, *"And just as Moses lifted up the serpent in the desert, so must the Son of Man be lifted up"* (John 3:14). Also, the Word of God entered the waters of creation on the first day when God said, *"Let there be light."* The light entered the waters and the darkness of the abyss, as Jesus' soul entered the abode of the dead when he died on the cross. On the second day of creation God said, *"Let there be a dome in the middle of the waters, to separate one body of water from the other."* On the seventh day of creation, God rested from all of his work. On the seventh day, Jesus' body rested in the tomb. We can compare his body to the dome or firmament on the second day of creation separating the waters above from the waters below where his soul had descended. Another image to consider is the angel who separated the Israelites in the Red Sea from Pharaoh's army. Jesus on the second day could easily separate those in prison from the oppressors that were keeping them in bondage. He gave light to those who were being saved and leaving the oppressors in darkness, therefore protecting those whom he was leading out of the abyss.

On the third day of creation God said, *"Let the water under the sky be gathered into a single basin, so that the dry land may appear."* From the dry land, the Lord said, *"Let the earth bring forth vegetation: every kind of plant that bears seed and every kind of fruit tree on earth that bears fruit with its seed in it."* This third day Jesus resurrected from the dead and the saints followed him into life. Jesus preached to the souls in prison, sowing the seed of the Word of God. Jesus brought the good news to the souls in prison that he came to set them free from bondage to the devil.

The Israelites found a pool of water after three days but the water was bitter. David and his men came back to their cities and their families had been taken captive. All those destined for heaven could reunite with Adam and Eve but our first parents were as a pool of bitter water. They could not give eternal life to themselves and they could not quench the thirst of their descendants. Suddenly on the third day, Jesus, sacrificed on the cross, was thrown into the bitter water. Jesus the son of David rescued the captives from the Amalekites. Suddenly the bitter water became sweet, and all the captives reunited with their husbands and their fathers. God quenched their thirst, because now they had life with God their Father, from whom they had been estranged since the sin of Adam and Eve. Jesus took the keys of death from Satan and opened the gates of heaven.

†

FORTY DAYS

Jesus resurrected from the dead on the third day. He conquered death; we have forgiveness for our sins and now can live forever with God in heaven. Is that all there is to it? Well, there is much more. Examining the contents of this book will lead one to see that Israel replaced Egypt in a priestly role, and David replaced Saul as King. Jesus Christ replaced Satan as the ruler of the world. Because Jesus is the Son of God, his Spirit is the Spirit of Truth and he has taken dominion from the father of lies. In the Incarnation, God became man, showing Jesus is the Son of Man. He is the prophet because he has a body to speak the word. As the Son of Man, he replaced Adam because from Adam when conceived we inherit original sin, and from Jesus, when we are baptized, we inherit the forgiveness of sins.

Israel and David foreshadowed Jesus, and in Jesus the offices of priest, prophet and king were united. Jesus is the High Priest, the Word of God, and the King of Kings. The resurrection reveals that Jesus conquered death, but the war is not over. As mentioned in the last chapter, that John the beloved disciple personified the tribe of Judah leading the other tribes in battle. We must now fight as if we do not know the outcome of the war, but be encouraged to persist. God and his military are victors in this war, because his Only Begotten Son has already defeated the enemy.

The historical facts remain true in the stories of Israel,

and David, and Jesus. Yet there is an allegorical side to these accounts in salvation history. Everyone who fights as an opponent to God and his plan of salvation may not understand the role they are playing. The Egyptians, Saul, the Jews, and the Romans are redeemable and God wants salvation for them. There is no redemption however for the gods of Egypt, Amalek, or the ruler of this world, Satan.

In the beginning, *the LORD God formed man out of the clay of the ground and blew into his nostrils the breath of life, and so man became a living being. The LORD God gave man this order: "You are free to eat from any of the trees in the garden except the tree of knowledge of good and bad. From that tree you shall not eat; the moment you eat from it you are surely doomed to die"* (Genesis 2:7, 16-17). In the creation account here, God did three things. First, came the conception of man, when the dust particles were made into a single being. Second, the man became a living being when God blew the breath of life into his nostrils. Third, God gave him what is needed to sustain life, which is something to eat. However, man must be free to choose and Adam had the choice between obedience and disobedience, which translates as life or death. God made man in his own image and the firstborn, Adam, was the son of God.

On the evening of the resurrection, Jesus made his apostles into his image. They are his firstborn. *On the evening of the first day of the week, when the doors were locked, where the disciples were, for fear of the Jews, Jesus came and stood in their midst and said to them, "Peace be with you"* (John 20:19-23). And with this phrase he united them and the apostles became one man. *He breathed on them and said to them, "Receive the*

Holy Spirit," and the man became a living being in Jesus' own image. *"Whose sins you forgive are forgiven them, and whose sins you retain are retained."* Again, there is the way to sustain life and the way to death. Thus, the bishop governs as a king who grants pardon and imposes penalties.

If there is any confusion about the apostles given authority to forgive sins there should not be, because Jesus also said, *"As the Father sent me, so I send you."* After which he repeated, *"Peace be with you,"* for a second time. Jesus sent his apostles to unite disciples with the Word of God, and the catechumens are taught the truth and brought into the body of Christ. This is the unity of the faith, which the Bishop speaks as prophet when he greets the congregation, "Peace be with you." The bishop is also high priest and he is father to the baptized in his diocese, because everyone who is baptized becomes a living being.

When Jesus referred to "those whose sins you forgive," he implied there must be a way to sustain life after baptism, and it is done by the confession of sins. This is how we keep the breath of life that made us living beings, by keeping our conscience clean. It must be different from the command given to the first man because he existed before sin was present in the world. Since we come into the world with the sin we inherited, we become a living being when this sin is forgiven. We remain a living being when we confess the sins we have committed after baptism. Everyone who confesses his sins has accepted being judged and no longer judges what is good or evil. Once an individual gives up the right to eat from the tree of knowledge of good and evil, he may then be allowed to eat from the tree of life because the bishop no longer retains his sins. This is one of the greatest gifts from God and one of the greatest mysteries of being in full communion with the Roman Catholic Church.

Jesus dwelled with his disciples for forty days before he ascended to heaven where he took his place at the right hand of the Father. During these forty days, the disciples of Jesus are like the Israelites in the desert. The church is the new Israel, living in an obscure place, apart from the world. The New Israel had God as their king for these forty days and, because of Jesus' obedience to God the Father, they did not spend forty years as the Israelites did in the desert. After forty days, Jesus ascended into heaven and left the disciples with the promise that he would send the Holy Spirit to teach and guide them.

Once the apostles received the Holy Spirit, they were persecuted by the Jews, as was Jesus. The disciples were faithful to the Word of God. They were treated with contempt, yet they resisted the temptation to reject the authority of the ministerial offices of priests, prophets, and kings.

The following chart begins with the failings of Israel in the desert and parallels King Saul in his three temptations. The same temptations seemed to destroy Israel and Judah both as nations. The Jews, being last to suffer these temptations, were also taken into a diaspora. Jesus subjected himself to humiliation and suffering in like manner, but, being without sin, he was able to withstand being tempted while remaining faithful to the Father.

This schematic chart compares Israel in the desert, and King Saul and his sons in relation to Israel, Judah and the Jews. These were the failures of those who rebelled against God.

ISRAEL IN THE DESERT – UNFAITHFUL TO THE LORD		
PRIESTS Tempted God and asked: "Is the Lord in our midst or not?"	PROPHETS Made the golden calf	KINGS Worshiped the gods of the other kingdoms

KING SAUL – UNFAITHFUL TO THE LORD		
Offered the holocaust, which only the priests were allowed to offer	Would not carry out the ban on Amalek as the Lord commanded	Practiced divination, by having a witch to conjure up a ghost for him
MALCHISHUA Killed by the Philistines	ABINADAB Killed by the Philistines	JONATHAN Killed by the Philistines
THE JEWS JUDGED BY PRIESTS Destroyed by the Romans	JUDAH JUDGED BY PROPHETS Destroyed by the Babylonians	ISRAEL JUDGED BY KINGS Destroyed by the Assyrians

This chart reveals the success of the Redeemer. Jesus avoided sin, even when he was tortured to death. The apostles and the faithful reveal the success of the redeemed, those who repent and call on the name of Jesus to be saved.

JESUS - FAITHFLUL TO THE FATHER (THE LAMB WITHOUT BLEMISH)		
PRIEST - SPIRIT *Tempted in the garden*	PROPHET - BODY *Scourged at the pillar*	KING - HEAD *Crowned with thorns*

ACTS OF THE APOSTLES - FAITHFUL TO JESUS		
PETER & JOHN	PETER, THE APOSTLES, & STEVEN	PETER & JAMES
PRIESTS *Tempted – never again speak to anyone in Jesus name*	PROPHETS *Apostles flogged, and Steven stoned to death*	KINGS *James beheaded, and Peter set free by the angel of the Lord*

Three Times
Set Apart

Seven Days of
Creation as in
Seven Chapters

The Sacrifice

The Acts of the Apostles

Saul Pursued Jesus

Crossed Over

Three-Day Journey

Forty Years

FOUR

†
Saul of Tarsus

THREE TIMES SET APART

I BEGAN WRITING ABOUT SAUL of Tarsus and took a tour through salvation history beginning with the Israelites as slaves in Egypt. By now it should be apparent that these stories are relevant to each other, and hopefully the evidence given was compelling enough to draw interest in the role that Saul of Tarsus played in the church. We today refer to him most commonly as St. Paul. I will use the name Saul of Tarsus, though not to distinguish who he was before canonization as a saint, but for consistency in accordance with the Holy Scriptures. Therefore, where Scripture refers to him as Saul I will use that name and where Scripture refers to him as Paul I will use that name. There is no evidence of a name change at any particular time as we can see in Acts 13:9: *But Saul also known as Paul, filled with the Holy Spirit.* I hope that this will not lead to confusion when the name St. Paul is used, as this is the name in which the church refers to him.

Saul was set apart, and he makes mention of being set apart at different times and in different ways. The first mention of he being set apart is in Acts 13:2: *the Holy Spirit said, "Set apart for me Barnabas and Saul for the work to which I have called them." Then completing their fasting and prayer they laid hands on them and sent them off.* Without trying to limit the importance of any other occasion when he was set apart, the discussion here will focus on three events.

The first way in which Saul was set apart was at birth. He received Roman citizenship when he was born because his father was a Roman citizen. Some sources say that the politician Anthony conferred Roman citizenship on all the inhabitants of Tarsus; the Emperor Caesar Augustus later ratified this. Roman citizenship was a privilege politically and culturally, especially since Jews generally were not allowed citizenship.

The second way in which Saul was set apart is when he was circumcised on the eighth day. He was a Hebrew of the tribe of Benjamin, and in circumcision he was set apart as a member of the people of God. They were a people set apart and peculiar, a holy nation and a kingdom of priests. He is a descendant of his father Abraham. Saul was brought up in the ways and customs of the Jewish people, in submission to Moses and the Law.

The third way in which Saul was set apart is when he became a Pharisee. The name Pharisee means righteous ones, holy ones set apart. Saul studied under Gamaliel, who was one of the most respected and revered teachers. Gamaliel was one of only seven Pharisees given the title Rabban, which demonstrates the high honor he held as a teacher. Saul referred to himself as a Pharisee and the son of Pharisees. He had Gamaliel as his father to teach him the interpretations of the Sacred Scriptures in the Hillel tradition.

Saul eventually came to the realization that God, who existed from all eternity, is his Father and had set him apart even before he was born. If one is set apart, that person is set apart for a purpose. There are not many things in life more valuable and more precious than finding one's purpose in life. Saul had that great blessing of knowing that he labored not in vain. He suffered much for the sake of Christ and the gospels, but his consolation was that he was allowed to join Christ in his suffering.

All this being true, it took time and effort for Saul to discover what purpose he was set apart for. His intellect and physical strength were exhausted in his zeal for Moses and the Law. He persecuted Jesus by trying to destroy the church. As many well intended individuals, he did not persecute the Christians out of evil desire, but to please God. Many of the Jews were convinced that Jesus was a blasphemer, and could not allow him to live. It was their duty to put away this evil or be punished by God. Saul of Tarsus continued to persecute Christians because now Jesus lived on in his disciples. The movement was gaining momentum and many Jews were beginning to follow the way.

Saul of Tarsus, like every one of us, was in need of conversion. To be convinced of one's holiness can be a snare. Boldness and tenacity are necessary when standing for truth. Yet divine revelation is received in humility and poverty, and it becomes the nourishment shared by those who embrace chastity and obedience. It was most difficult for those under the Law to understand spiritual things because the Old Covenant was in the flesh. Therefore, Saul of Tarsus was able to see that he was set apart in three ways, because he followed the way of his fathers. However, each way he was set apart was in the flesh. All that was missing was the Spirit that gives life to the flesh. He continued in the way of his fathers, because he desired to fulfill all righteousness, but after his conversion he realized that something crucial had been missing.

†

SEVEN DAYS OF CREATION AS IN SEVEN CHAPTERS

The church is the New Israel and thus it is a new creation. The Genesis accounts of creation are present throughout the Bible. Saul of Tarsus' life moved from being set apart three times into the battle between Christianity and Judaism. Let's review the seven days of the new creation as seven days in which Saul of Tarsus was in battle with his enemies. The battle was fierce and it seemed he was losing, but he was determined to hold out because he was fighting for Israel and for the God of Israel. Each day of creation was a blow of defeat to Judaism. Saul and the Jewish leaders were fighting to preserve the only true religion given to a people set apart by the only true God. They fought against the gentiles, because the gentiles wished to impose their religious beliefs and gods on the Jews. However, this fight was a civil war among Jews who intended to preserve, protect and defend the deposit of faith, which was the Law given through Moses. Saul and the Jewish leaders perceived the Christians as Jews who were perverting Judaism.

With each day of creation, another level was constructed. When seven levels were completed, the construction of the tower would be complete. Saul's determination was the destruction of this tower. I am speaking in terms of comparing the building of the church to the creation account in Genesis 1. It may also help to illustrate how the Jewish authorities viewed the apostles as a threat to their authority. An ecclesial hierarchy was being established to replace the Jewish religious authorities and the Jews had to prevent this from happening.

First day of creation – *"Let there be light."* One might wonder what darkness we are trying to dispel. For one, the tragic loss of one of the disciples, Judas Iscariot, was a sad event. Peter even referred to the Scriptures: "For it is written in the Book of Psalms, *'Let his encampment become desolate, and may no one dwell in it.'* And *'May another take his office'*" (Acts 1:20). And now to add to their sorrows, Jesus was about to ascend to heaven and leave the apostles here in the world. To console them Jesus said, *"John baptized with water, but in a few days you will be baptized with the Holy Spirit."* When Jesus gave this great commission, his words entered the place of darkness and desolation. At this point the Word of God entered the disciples as on the first day of creation when God said, *"Let there be light."* The Word of God entered the waters, which covered the darkness of the abyss, and the light entered the darkness. The disciples waited then in joyful hope, because their darkness and desolation had been changed to light and consolation. They were fully aware that Jesus could be trusted and everything he promised would happen.

Second day of creation -*"Let there be a dome in the middle of the waters to separate the waters above the dome from the waters below the dome."* Peter exercised authority as high priest and sought instructions from the Lord by drawing lots. The sorrow of losing Judas Iscariot was changed into joyful hope and God chose Matthias to replace Judas. On the day of Pentecost, the Holy Spirit descended on the church in the upper room. The upper room became the dome that separated the waters of heaven and earth, dividing the waters above from the waters below. It was the heavens as much as Jesus in his mother's womb and Jesus' body in the tomb separated the waters above from the waters below. The upper room, like the sky, contained what was needed to breathe. The Holy Spirit came in as the sound of rushing wind, because the Holy Spirit is the breath who makes an individual come alive. About three thousand were baptized that day and each became a living being.

Devout Jews from every nation under heaven were in Jerusalem to experience the defeat of Babylon. When men were building a tower to heaven, the Lord confused their languages and they were scattered into the nations. Here the Lord was building the tower to heaven, and he brought the devout Jews from all the nations to hear his voice. As Jesus said, *"Everyone who belongs to the truth hears my voice."* They heard the apostles and understood them in their language. There is one Spirit of Truth and no confusion.

Third day of creation – *"Let the earth bring forth vegetation: every kind of plant that bears seed and every kind of fruit tree on earth that bears fruit with its seed in it."* The man crippled from birth could not enter the temple because of his infirmity. Peter gave him his right hand and raised him up from the earth. The man entered the temple walking and jumping, praising God. He received a new body similar to those who followed Jesus out of the graves. The seed is the Word of God and he was born into new life, freed from the oppression of the evil one. The man was set free from the earth to rise up into the dome of the sky and breathe freely the Spirit of God. When Peter addressed the people among the things he said was, *"You denied the Holy and righteous One and asked that a murderer be released to you. The author of life you put to death, but God raised him from the dead, of this we are witnesses."* The construction of God's tower continued with the resurrection of Jesus' body from the tomb, fulfilling what Jesus said, *"Destroy this temple and I will raise it in three days."* Here on the third day of this new creation of the church, the crippled man was raised from the earth.

Fourth day of creation – *"Let there be lights in the dome of the sky, to separate day from night."* In creation, God created the greater light, the lesser light and the stars to serve as luminaries. The greater light, the sun, shines forth and gives us the light of day, but the lesser light reflects the light from the sun and does not give light without the sun. Thus, the sun is necessary for the light of day and for the lesser light to illuminate the night.

The fourth chapter of Acts begins with Peter and John still speaking to the people when the priests, the captain of the temple guard, and the Sadducees confronted them. They were disturbed because Peter and John were teaching the people and proclaiming in Jesus the resurrection of the dead. Peter and John were arrested but many of those who heard the word came to believe and the number of men grew to about five thousand.

The Jewish leaders, elders, and scribes were assembled in Jerusalem, with Annas the high priest, Caiaphas, John, Alexander, and all who were of the high-priestly class. They questioned Peter and John: *"By what power or by what name have you done this?"* Then Peter filled with the Holy Spirit answered them. Yet, when they ordered Peter and John not to speak or teach at all in the name of Jesus. Peter and John replied, *"Whether it is right in the sight of God for us to obey you rather than God, you be the judges"* (Acts 4:19). Peter spoke alone as one filled with the Holy Spirit, but Peter and John spoke together. In this new creation, they are as the sun and moon, the greater and the lesser light. When Peter and John returned to their own people, the whole community raised their voices with one accord and said, *"Sovereign Lord, maker of heaven and earth and the sea and all that is in them"* (Acts 4:24). The whole community prayed this prayer as the stars of heaven praising God.

Fifth day of creation – *"Let the water teem with an abundance of living creatures, and on the earth let birds fly beneath* *the dome of the sky."* Jesus building his church sent the Holy Spirit to unite the members of the church and make them one body. The Holy Spirit is the soul of the church, and they have all things in common because they are of one Spirit. Their material possessions are not as important and only serve to represent what they are spiritually; a community of one heart and mind.

Ananias and Sapphira lied to the Holy Spirit, and both fell dead. The first indication of excommunication occurred when a deceitful spirit tried to enter the church. The Spirit of Truth has nothing in common with the father of lies, and in Jesus' words, *"The ruler of this world will be driven out"* (John 12:31). Ananias and Sapphira along with the deceiving spirit were cast out of the dome of the sky into the water below.

The apostles were imprisoned for their good works. People brought their sick and those disturbed by unclean spirits and all were cured. The high priest and all his companions were filled with jealousy. They laid hands upon the apostles and put them in jail. Peter and the apostles replied to their charges, "We must obey God rather than men." Again, they spoke as one. The angel of the Lord had let them out of prison and although the Sanhedrin wanted to put them to death, Gamaliel talked them out of it. The apostles were flogged and released as birds set free from the snare of a fowler, free to fly beneath the dome of the sky. Great numbers were added to them.

Sixth day of creation – *"Let us make man in our image, after our likeness."* The apostles needed ministers to help with the daily distribution. In the sixth chapter of John, Jesus needed ministers to help distribute the bread and fish to the multitude. He made the apostles in his image when giving them this task. Created in Jesus' image, they are not equal to Jesus because Jesus is God. Jesus himself said, *"If you loved me, you would rejoice that I am going to the Father, for the Father is greater than I"* (John 14:28). Although Jesus is God, as the image of God he emptied himself and took the form of a slave. "The seven" are servants made in the image of the apostles. The apostles are greater than the seven even though all of them are human. The high priest and those of the high-priestly class rejected the apostles and with good reason. The apostles are bishops and, therefore, high priests themselves. Christians have a new priesthood and a new sacrifice. This new priesthood and sacrifice will replace Levites and the animal sacrifices. To compound the frustration and fears of the Sadducees, a large number of priests had also become obedient to the Christian faith.

Seventh day of creation – *Since on the seventh day God was finished with the work he had been doing, he rested on the seventh day from all the work he had undertaken.* At the end of the seventh chapter, Steven fell asleep. God completed the tower to heaven, and the first martyr, Steven reached the top of the tower into heaven. Why was Steven martyred? Because enemies of the church were trying to destroy the temple, Jesus' body. They brought in false witnesses against Stephen, and their lies were similar to the accusations made against Jesus. Every prophet who submits to Jesus and the authority Jesus established is a true prophet. When Steven was on trial before the Sanhedrin high court, he gave a discourse, which summarized salvation history beginning with Abraham and ending with Jesus. He said to them "Your ancestors murdered the prophets and you killed Jesus, the Son of God." This type of revelation, even if from God, is more than anyone can bear. Only someone who is ready to die will accept being judged. The person who accepts death will rise with Christ, but these people were not ready for conversion, and, as in the past, the prophet must die. The prophet must die because he exposes them to the light. The light reveals their deeds and their thoughts, which they prefer to remain in darkness. The only solution for those not willing or able to repent is to extinguish the light by killing the prophet. They justified their actions by reasoning if the prophet was of God, then God would not have let this happen to him. Steven accused them, yet he forgave them. He labored and then he fell asleep on the Sabbath; he entered God's rest.

THE SACRIFICE

At Steven's execution, the witnesses laid down their cloaks at the feet of a young man named Saul. The Israelites laid their cloaks before Jesus on Palm Sunday, when they accepted him as King. Perhaps it was a gesture that they accepted Saul as a true prophet as opposed to Steven, whom they viewed as a false prophet. Now Saul was consenting to his execution. Saul described himself later as a Pharisee and as one who surpassed his brothers in zeal for the Law. If Saul was a scribe, then he was a prophet, and would not want to be replaced by deacons. After all Saul studied with Gamaliel, who was one of "the seven" scribes with the highest honor given the title Rabban. Why should they be replaced by "the seven," who are the lowest of servants?

There is another reason why Saul consented to Steven's execution. Saul realized that the men were slipping away from him. Does this sound familiar? King Saul had the same concern. This is about how to worship. Saul of Tarsus approved of Steven being stoned to death because after seven days of battle he attempted to win the Lord's favor. The first martyrdom in the church fulfilled Jesus' prophecy: *They will expel you from the synagogues; in fact, the hour is coming when everyone who kills you will think he is offering worship to God* (John 16:1). Saul's approval of Steven's execution was no more acceptable than King Saul offering the holocaust. Both committed an offense against the Law. The stoning of Steven is an unacceptable sacrifice, because Steven is a true prophet, and it is a grave injustice to judge and condemn a person for speaking the truth. Thus, Saul continued the work of his ancestors who killed the prophets.

What makes it so difficult for the people of God to move forward when God gives them hope for salvation? Why are they satisfied with their status even when surrounded by disaster? While I do not believe there is a simple explanation that will suffice, we must look at the seven deadly sins to penetrate deeper into this mystery. We become attached to sins and the pleasures derived from a sinful state of being.

For example, there appears to be three times in salvation

history when God changed the way we worship. Each time God came to us and determined what was necessary for the salvation of humanity. The first indication of this was when Adam and Eve sinned. They were no longer in the state of original innocence and justice in which God created them. Before committing the original sin, they were justified by their innocence. After sinning, God provided a plan of salvation that required repentance. When God questioned them, it became obvious they would not repent. Instead, they looked back to their original state and claimed to be not guilty because of illegal entrapment. The woman claimed to be justified because she was deceived, thus she is no more culpable than an insane person is. Without repentance, God had to change their worship, and they were no longer allowed to eat from the tree of life. What made all of this possible were lust, greed, and gluttony; the tree was beautiful to look at, and its fruit was good for food. Even though they had all the other trees in the garden for food, they were not satisfied and desired more.

 When God saved the Israelites from slavery in Egypt, he brought them into the desert and gave them the Law. The Law requires animal sacrifice and when Moses came down the mountain with the commandments and the rules of ritual sacrifice, the people had already made a golden calf. The sin that lead them into slavery was the rejection of the prophet Joseph. They gave away their gold to feed their bellies, and they were saved from starvation. By selling the prophet into slavery, they sold themselves into slavery. God gave them a new sacrifice for their salvation in the Law, but they looked back to how they were saved from starvation by offering Pharaoh their gold. They offered their gold in the fire as an attempt to find their way back to Canaan.

The patriarchs would not follow Joseph the prophet because of jealousy. Their father favored Joseph, and Joseph had the gift of prophecy. They would have killed him to take the gift from him, but settled for selling him into slavery in Egypt. Envy and anger seems to be the motivation and driving force behind their actions. If the descendants of the patriarchs could accept the prophets God sent them, maybe there would be no need for the Law. However the children of Israel are like their fathers, the patriarchs, and were unwilling to repent. They continued in their stubbornness, rebellion, persecution and murder. Envy and anger remains a fire that burns within.

One last time God changed the way that we worship when Jesus gave the Eucharist. He offered himself as a ransom for the people of God, but they rejected this offer and looked back to how their ancestors were saved by the Law. They rejected the prophets as much as their ancestors did, but God had determined it was the time to fulfill the promise made to Abraham. God is faithful and does not deceive. Jesus revealed the true God to reconcile humanity with God. We have not trusted God since the devil said, *"You certainly will not die! No, God knows well that the moment you eat of it your eyes will be opened and you will be like gods who know what is good and what is bad"* (Genesis 3:4-5).

Why then was it so difficult for humanity to move forward and offer a new sacrifice, or accept a new way of worshiping? Because it would be an admission of guilt. For people to move forward, there must be repentance of evils present and past. Repentance frees us from the shackles of slavery. In the case of spiritual slavery, the first step to emancipation would be to recognize that one is enslaved. The Jews of Jesus' time did not appear to be ready to move forward to where Jesus was leading them, and it was mostly because of distrust.

To move from the covenant in the flesh to the new covenant, which is internal, one must put away the things of the flesh. It is a transfer of power from the old man Adam, to the new man Jesus. The old man Adam is powerless and his descendants are enslaved to the devil, yet the people suspected Jesus was trying to gain dominion over them. How do you convince people that they are enslaved when they maintain that they are free? Eve led Adam to eat the forbidden fruit. Israel led Aaron to make the golden calf. The Jews tempted Jesus to come down from the cross. It appears the people of God were slothful about spiritual things and tried to hold on to Moses and the Law, because the Law governed the flesh. They did not want their thoughts to be judged and this is where Jesus was leading them. The sins of Adam and Eve, Israel, and the Jews of Jesus' time are no different from our sins. Pride is at the root of all the deadly sins, whether greed, lust, anger, envy, gluttony, or sloth, and the cause of pride is the lie.

†

SAUL PURSUED JESUS

After the martyrdom of Steven, there was a severe persecution of the church in Jerusalem. Saul tried to destroy the church, entering house after house, dragging out men and women, and delivering them to prison. What is it that caused Saul to breathe murderous threats against the disciples of the Lord and drag them back to Jerusalem in chains? I believe that Saul of Tarsus personifies a group within the people of God. He has been reconciled with God and returned to a place of honor. He served the Lord with dignity and with intense love and obedience. Unfortunately, it is necessary that we view the unpleasant saga of rebellion, caused by sin and the darkness of ignorance, to arrive at the beautiful destination of the third heaven Saul experienced.

Saul of Tarsus was an Israelite from the tribe of Benjamin. The war against Christianity was more about hostility between Judah and Benjamin. King Saul, the first king of Israel spent his life trying to kill David. He did not want his servant David to become king. The kingdom as taken from Saul's descendants represents the death of the firstborn. Even after the death of King Saul, the tribe of Benjamin would not accept David as King. It would take seven and a half years before David would rule over the whole of Israel. This story foreshadowed the battle between Christ and the Jews. Jesus was referred to by some of the people as Son of David. He is the Son of David to whom the eternal throne was promised. By the time the people accepted Jesus as King on Palm Sunday, the Jewish leaders were ready to do anything to stop Jesus. After Jesus raised Lazarus and made his entry into Jerusalem, the crowd went to meet him because they heard that he had done this sign. *"So the Pharisees said to one another, "You see that you are gaining nothing. Look, the whole world has gone after him"* (John 12:19).

When the kingdom was taken from King Saul, it was taken from the tribe of Benjamin. The servant had become king, because David was a man after God's own heart and he would carry out all of God's commands. King Saul had three sons who were killed in battle by the Philistines. One of his sons, Jonathan, supported David. Later in history, the Assyrians destroyed the nation of Israel. The Babylonians destroyed Judah as a nation. Once the people returned from Babylon, they were called Jews. Benjamin, because of its proximity to Judah and the temple, and because they practiced Judaism, were considered Jews by default.

Saul of Tarsus was of the tribe of Benjamin and he was opposed to Jesus, the Son of David. Jesus was the Servant, but he was later exalted as King. The kingdom was not taken from the family of Saul of Tarsus. What was taken from Saul of Tarsus was the authority to teach. He was a Pharisee who studied with the prestigious Gamaliel. The scribes were teachers of the Law, and to them Jesus was abolishing the Law. Jesus, however, explained that he did not come to abolish the Law, but to fulfill it. Still, Saul and the Jews felt they were being stripped of their place of honor and prestige as teachers of the Law. Jesus was crucified, but his disciples were freeing

Jews from their obligation to keep the Law. To Saul, Jesus and his disciples were replacing Moses and the Law with a new teaching. The Jews have lost their place of honor as the chosen people of God. Even the gentiles are welcomed in this new temple. This puts the tribe of Benjamin and the tribe of Judah at odds again. Saul of Tarsus persecuted Christ in the same manner that King Saul persecuted David.

Jesus came to free the captives, not only from slavery to the devil, but also from slavery to the Law. Those who felt the oppression of a spiritual slavery cried out to Jesus sometimes with statements such as, *"Jesus, Son of David have pity on me"* (Luke 18:38). These people were more than happy to be set free.

Jesus gave an example describing the hypocrisy of the scribes and the Pharisees. *"They tie up heavy burdens [hard to carry] and lay them on people's shoulders, but they will not lift a finger to move them"* (Matthew 23:4). These were burdens added to the Law in the traditions of the elders. Why did God give them the Law if the Law was slavery? It was for a people who were not ready to receive the Spirit. They were tired of the physical slavery in Egypt, but not ready to submit spiritually to the prophet.

Jesus freed those who were willing to be emancipated spiritually. He delivered them from possession, oppression, the physical effects from spiritual attacks, and enslavement. Israel was enslaved spiritually while continuing to worship the God of Abraham, Isaac, and Jacob. How can this be? It has to do with what Samuel told King Saul, *"Rebellion is like divination."* Saul continued to serve the Lord and even tried to justify his disobedience, maintaining that he obeyed the Lord. He persisted in trying to kill David, although David was the only person that could free Saul from the torment of the evil spirit. The Jews were living that same experience. Only Jesus could free them from the torments of the devil and the unclean spirits. The Jewish leaders put up the same type of resistance to Jesus that the Pharaoh and King Saul did to the Lord.

†

CROSSED OVER INTO THE THREE-DAY JOURNEY

Now Saul, still breathing murderous threats against the disciples of the Lord, went to the high priest and asked him for letters to the synagogues in Damascus that if he should find any men or women who belonged to the Way, he might bring them back to Jerusalem in chains. On his journey, as he was nearing Damascus, a light from the sky flashed around him. He fell to the ground and heard a voice saying to him, "Saul, Saul, why are you persecuting me? He said, "Who are you sir?" The reply came, "I am Jesus whom you are persecuting. Now get up and go into the city and you will be told what you must do" (Acts 9:1-6).

Saul was on his way to Damascus in pursuit of Jesus' followers. The way to Damascus became the Red Sea for him. God gave him a glance and it blinded him. The glance God gave to Pharaoh's army kept them from finding their way out of the Red Sea. The glance that God gave to the men of Sodom blinded them and kept them from finding their way out of the city when it was destroyed. God instructed Saul, however, to go into the city where he would be told what to do. Saul will later testify to the grace and mercy of God, because he knows from experience.

When the Lord stopped speaking to King Saul because of his disobedience, Saul was desperate to find out what he must do. So desperate was he that he turned to a witch to use divination. His hope was that Samuel's ghost would tell him what he must do. The Lord gave no instructions to King Saul and he perished along with his sons at the hands of the Philistines. About a millennium later, the Lord finally spoke to Saul, but a different Saul. A mighty warrior from the tribe of Benjamin, although he led the fight in a different type of war, Saul of Tarsus heard what King Saul longed to hear. He received instructions from the Lord. It was necessary that Saul became blind, because he is a descendant of Adam and Eve and his eyes were open. Jesus said that he came so that the blind might see and those who see might become blind. Saul witnessed the resurrected Christ and crossed over into the spiritual realm. At this point Saul had to experience his own death, and he had to come through the darkness.

For three days, he was unable to see, and he neither ate nor drank. During this time, Saul was praying. When Ananias entered the house and laid hands on him, he said, *"Saul, my brother, the Lord has sent me, Jesus who appeared to you on the way by which you came, that you may regain your sight and be filled with the Holy Spirit. "Immediately things like scales fell from his eyes and he regained his sight. He got up and was baptized, and when he had eaten, he recovered his strength"* (Acts 9:17-19).

A thousand years had passed before another leader of Benjamin named Saul received instructions from the Lord about what he must do. And the same amount of time had passed since an Egyptian; a slave of an Amalekite was brought to David. This man fell ill and his master abandoned him. He went three days and three nights, and he neither ate nor drank. David and his men gave him something to eat and he led them to the Amalekite raiding party. David recovered all the prisoners. The Egyptian was part of the raiding parting at first, but later he led David to the camp of the Amalekites so that David could take back his plunder.

This is also what Saul of Tarsus did. He was like the Egyptian, who was a slave of an Amalekite, because he was with the raiding parties that took Jesus' family captive. Once Saul was baptized, ate, and recovered his strength, he led the way in helping Jesus take back his plunder. Jesus, son of David recovered everything that belonged to him and nothing was lost. After the three-day journey, Saul of Tarsus found life, and the life he found was in Christ. He no longer lives for himself but for Christ who lives in him.

†

FORTY YEARS

The forty-year period in Scripture is both literal and symbolic. In this chapter, the meaning has been restricted to a symbolic term. Most certainly, there is a constant struggle in life, and that struggle is against death. From the time of conception until birth, an infant struggles to enter life outside of the womb. This period is represented as a forty-week pregnancy. Birth may come sooner or later than the forty weeks. Nonetheless, forty years is symbolic here of Paul's life from baptism until martyrdom. His struggle for life began with baptism and ended when he was put to death, although death here means born into new life.

In the first twelve chapters of the Book of Acts, the infant church was struggling for life also. The church had joined Jesus in his suffering. During this time, in the ninth chapter, Saul of Tarsus was converted and began to preach Jesus Christ resurrected. The confrontation between life and death continued as the infant church grew and matured. The disciples were persecuted by the Jewish authorities, yet the church continued to grow in number. The most stunning example of fidelity to Jesus was the willingness of the apostles to suffer for Jesus' name and the sake of the gospel. The Holy Spirit gave the apostles and all faithful disciples the fortitude needed to stand up for the truth even in the face of death. Their sufferings mirror that of Jesus' suffering, and the disciples were drawn into the Passion of Christ. It is with great honor that they accepted suffering for Jesus' name, perhaps in the realization that this level of contemplation drew them closer to a perfect union with Jesus.

The following chart reflects how Jesus began to build his church as a new creation. This new creation is also the building of a tower to heaven. The tower that men tried to build after the flood in Genesis 11 was destroyed, and all of humanity was scattered among the nations. Their languages were confused so that they could not understand one another. This was done to limit the evil that humanity could accomplish and it limited pride. The tower that God is building in the book of Acts is the true tower to heaven. This tower is the church of Jesus Christ, built on the rock of Peter.

Note that each time Peter preached, the number of disciples grew and the base of the tower expanded. In the sixth chapter of Acts, the apostles realized the need to make servants in their image. They needed help with the distribution as Jesus did in the sixth chapter of John. The church chose "the seven," to help with this task, and after Steven was martyred, all disciples left Jerusalem except the apostles. The Word of God began to spread outside of Jerusalem by the disciples who were scattered because of the persecution. The multitudes scattered in the land of Babylon, whose languages are confused by the many spirits, will have the opportunity to become the people of God. The Spirit of Truth, the Spirit of the one true God, unites them in love.

THE LORD IS BUILDING A TOWER TO HEAVEN. HE BROUGHT THEM OUT OF BABYLON AND GAVE THEM ONE LANGUAGE; THE SPIRIT OF TRUTH			
THOSE OUTSIDE IN BABYLON	**MEDIATORS**	**JESUS BUILDING HIS CHURCH**
CHAPTER 1 - Judas, the guide, went ahead of Jesus. "Let his encampment become desolate, and may no one dwell in it."	Peter spoke, "Let another take his place."	There are 12 Apostles once Matthias replaced Judas. He followed Jesus from the beginning. About 120 disciples in the upper room.
CHAPTER 2 - Jews and converts to Judaism from every nation under heaven.	Peter spoke, "Repent and be baptized, every one of you, in the name of Jesus Christ for the forgiveness of your sins."	Those who accepted his message were baptized, and about 3000 persons were added that day.
CHAPTER 3 - A crippled man who begged for alms outside the temple at the beautiful gate.	Peter said, "In the name of Jesus Christ the Nazorean, rise and walk."	The man entered the temple and clung to Peter and John.
CHAPTER 4 – All the people hurried in amazement toward them in the portico called "Solomon's Portico"	Peter addressed the people that it is by faith in Jesus this man is healed.	Many of those who heard the word came to believe and the number of men grew to about 5000.

CHAPTER 5 - The sick and those disturbed by unclean spirits were brought to the apostles.	They even carried the sick out into the streets so that when Peter came by, at least his shadow might fall on one or another of them.	More than ever, believers in the Lord, great numbers of men and women were added to them.
CHAPTER 6 - The Hellenist complained their widows were being neglected in the daily distribution.	The 12 Apostles called together the community of disciples and said to them, "Select from among you 7 reputable men."	The Word of God continued to spread, and the number of the disciples in Jerusalem increased greatly; even a large group of priests were becoming obedient to the faith.
CHAPTER 7 - False witnesses were presented to testify against Steven.	Steven said, "I see the heavens opened and the Son of Man standing at the right hand of God."	Steven said, "Lord do not hold this sin against them; and he fell asleep." He entered God's rest.

Steven is martyred: the blood of the martyrs is seed for the church.

On that day, there broke out a severe persecution of the church in Jerusalem, and all were scattered throughout the countryside of Judea and Samaria, except the apostles. Now those who had been scattered went about preaching the word.

This chart reflects the seven days of creation and how God is building a tower to heaven. I wanted to revisit this theme to point out something very important about St. Paul. It is true that once the disciples left Jerusalem, Saul went after them to bring them back in chains. His behavior can be compared to that of the Pharaoh, who chased the Israelites into the Red Sea. He can be compared to King Saul, who chased David into the Philistine army. However, what is most important is that Jesus converted Saul of Tarsus, and, once converted, he submitted to the teaching authority of the church. He went to Peter and the other apostles for their approval of his teaching and ministry. His humility is demonstrated by this simple gesture. Saul was a bold and aggressive person, yet he was very humble before the truth, and it is because he understood that God is truth.

Jesus gave authority to the apostles to judge the twelve tribes of Israel. He gave Peter the keys to the kingdom and the power to bind and loose. St. Paul subjected himself to the authority of the church and remained in communion with Peter and the apostles. Jesus sent Saul to the church to regain his sight. Yes, he was called, but this call was to repentance. The call was, "Saul, Saul, why do you persecute me?" This is a call to repentance. Jesus sent him to the church to regain his sight. Acts 9 explains his conversion experience.

During this time Peter was passing through every region. He healed a paralytic named Aeneas, and restored Tabitha to life, and in Acts 10 Peter preached to the gentiles. He preached to Cornelius the centurion and his whole household was converted. *While Peter was still speaking these things, the Holy Spirit fell upon all who were listening to the word. The circumcised believers who had accompanied Peter were astounded that the gift of the Holy Spirit should have been poured out on the Gentiles also, for they could hear them speaking in tongues and glorifying God. Then Peter responded,*

"Can anyone withhold the water for baptizing these people, who have received the Holy Spirit even as we have?" (Acts 10:44-46).

Peter preached at Pentecost to Jews and converts to Judaism from every nation under heaven. *Those who accepted his message were baptized, and about three thousand persons were added that day* (Acts 2:41). The nations are a reference to the Greeks or those in the diaspora.

Peter preached in the temple. *"Many of those who heard the word came to believe and the number of men grew to about five thousand"* (Acts 4:4). They represent the Hebrews, because Hebrew was the official language.

Now in Caesarea there was a man named Cornelius, a centurion of the Cohort called the Italica, devout and God-fearing along with his whole household (Acts 10:1). When these people were converted through the preaching of Peter, Greek, Hebrew, and Latin were united. The church is now one, Jews and Gentiles alike. The universality of the church began with the preaching of Peter. The Holy Spirit unites all members of the church as one family. We remain united by love, and only love can hold a family together. The church is called "Catholic" because it is a universal kingdom.

St. Paul never rejected the authority of Peter and the other apostles who were in union with Peter. St. Paul did not start a separate church in which its members would have to choose between the authority of Peter or Paul. St. Paul respected the authority of Sacred Tradition and Sacred Scripture. St. Paul is the great scribe, and in a mysterious way represents the authority of Sacred Scripture, but he did not separate himself from the authority of Sacred Tradition represented by St. Peter and those in union with him.

I thought it important to mention these things because I know of many Catholics who are not at peace, mainly because they have imposed the burden of interpreting the Scriptures for themselves and will not listen to the church. Children are at peace and are not ashamed of their nakedness mainly because they are innocent. They inherit the original sin, but they are free to love because they accept the authority of their parents. Children are dependent on their parents for all sustenance and they are not ashamed of this dependence. Children rely on their parents to provide for their needs, whether physical, emotional, or spiritual and this makes it easy for them to accept the authority of their parents.

This is what Jesus explained when he said we must become as little children. God is our Father and the Church is our mother. She is given the responsibility and authority to teach and govern children as in any common household. The turmoil of today and other times in history is caused by children who claim that they are grown and do not have to live by the rules laid out by the parents, yet they refuse to leave home and begin to govern their own household. They choose to stay at home and live as delinquent juveniles. We must pray for the conversion of the world, but it is first important that we, as Catholic Christians, become little children. Unless this happens, we will betray the mission of Christ and the good news becomes a tool used to enslave others. St. Paul recognized these things; it is obvious by his writings. He recognized that Jesus called him, but it was a call to repentance. Jesus sent him to the church to regain his sight and the church sent him to evangelize. His missionary efforts were not independent of the church.

After the first twelve chapters of the Book of Acts, the role of Saul of Tarsus changes. The Holy Spirit instructed the leaders in the church to set apart Barnabas and Saul for a purpose that the Spirit would send them. They prayed and laid hands on the two and sent them off. From that time on, in the thirteenth chapter of Acts, Saul is referred to as Paul.

Being sent by the Holy Spirit, Paul realized his purpose for being brought into this world. He said God set him apart even before he was born. He followed Jesus in his suffering because that is what he was called to do. In Damascus, he prayed and waited to be told what to do, which was to suffer for Jesus' name. Paul answered his call faithfully, even to the point of death at the hands of the Roman government.

What does suffering for the sake of Jesus name accomplish? Jesus already died for our sins, he resurrected from the dead, and is in heaven preparing a place for us when we die. So what need is there for more suffering? These are questions that people wrestle with today as in the past. What is the meaning of a suffering church? The Roman Catholic Church has accepted the concept that we are a suffering church, and she teaches her members to embrace everything that is from God. However, it is difficult in our discernment to know always what God permits and what God would like to free us from. Many of the saints entered into a perfect union with God by being united with Jesus in his Passion.

I will speak, however, as to why I believe a suffering

church is necessary. The Catholic Church explains that because Jesus, the head of the church, accepted suffering and death, then we, the members of the body, must follow him in all things, and this includes suffering and death. Scripture said that Jesus was made perfect by suffering in obedience. This brings up another question, "If he was already perfect, how could he be made perfect?" One way of answering this question is that Jesus is perfect because he is God. He is also man without sin, and that makes him perfect, but, because he was man, he could be tempted.

Like the first man, Adam, who was created in perfect innocence, Jesus was incarnate in perfect innocence. Jesus suffered and remained innocent, and therefore he was tested and made perfect. You might say proven perfect in the sense that he is God. The innocence proved that God cannot deceive nor can he be deceived. Thereby God was reconciled with man, and the lie, which the devil told our first parents Adam and Eve, has been disproved. When the serpent accused the Almighty God of deceiving Adam and Eve about dying if they ate the fruit of the tree of knowledge of good and evil, this lie was perpetuated until Jesus reconciled humanity with God.

Jesus suffered to free us from *eternal* suffering. He did not free us from *temporal* suffering. Justice will be served and there is still punishment for sin. Yet, the punishment does not satisfy God in the sense that our suffering pleases him. The suffering is to change us and make us perfect. What pleases God is that we are made perfect, as he is perfect. Since nothing can be added to perfection, the treasures are stored up for others. We call this stored up treasure "the treasury of merit."

Jesus and all the saints who are made perfect contribute to this treasury. This includes St. Paul, who was willing to bear the marks of Christ in his suffering.

He bore the suffering in real time, thus he bore the marks of Christ. The suffering church is necessary because even when Jesus proved that God is trustworthy, people continue to distrust God. People remain subject to the devil, not willing to change, many times being convinced of their own goodness, therefore ruling out the possibility of conversion. This is where the suffering church fulfills her role, and that is for the conversion of sinners. To sum up the meaning of this type of suffering in one word it is, "love." Christ suffered because he loves us, and his temporal suffering freed us from eternal suffering. But the church and her members are commissioned to suffer for the conversion of souls. Our temporal suffering is to help others to reconcile with the Spirit of Truth, and this temporal suffering frees others from eternal estrangement from the kingdom of God.

St. Paul went to the synagogues in every city and preached Jesus Christ resurrected. The Jews throughout the empire received the opportunity to hear the gospel. When it was not received as good news, it was not the fault of St. Paul. He suffered such things as whippings, imprisonments, stonings, several assassination attempts, and shipwrecks. Everywhere he met hardships, but he fought a good fight. Like David, he became a man after God's own heart and he carried out God's every command.

St. Paul is the converted Saul of Tarsus, but he is more than that. The tribe of Benjamin has been restored to its place of honor. In Egypt, when Joseph reunited with his brothers, they sat and ate a meal. *When they were seated by his instructions according to their age, from the oldest to the youngest, they looked at one another in amazement; and as portions were brought to them from Joseph's table, Benjamin's portion was five times as large as anyone else's* (Genesis 43:33). Again, Benjamin received more than his brothers and Saul's conversion represents the conversion of his people.

Christians today must study the life of St. Paul. The story of the Jews is the story of the world. We are the people who rejected Jesus, and we are the people scattered in a diaspora. The Jews are God's chosen people to whom he chose to reveal himself. It also means that they suffered much for the salvation of the rest of the world. They suffered much for God's presence to remain among the nations. Now it is our time to accept suffering by making God present to those who refuse to submit to the Spirit of Truth. They deserve to know the truth, because the truth will make them free. As for us, our suffering will make us perfect.

Also by Deacon Norman Alexander:

The Hidden Life of Jesus

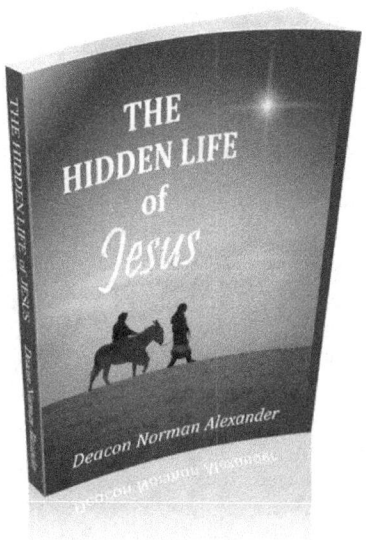

The Hidden Life of Jesus, by Deacon Norman Alexander, is a book that invites its readers to journey through crucial historical moments. Have you ever considered the relationship between Adam, Cain, and Enoch to the life of Moses? We are all aware that Moses is a type of Christ, but here you will see Salvation History unfold in ways not commonly spoken of. The parallels in the life of Moses and Jesus are intriguing and absolutely astonishing. God is truly the Author of history, as he takes the evil deeds of men and accomplishes good from them.

The Hidden Life of Jesus is Marian and its content emphasizes the importance of the role of our Blessed Mother. We must imitate her by exposing Jesus. That is our call; he must not remain hidden.

www.ingramcontent.com/pod-product-compliance
Lightning Source LLC
Chambersburg PA
CBHW072045290426
44110CB00014B/1574